HAMBURGER
★★★★MAGIC★★★

Publications International, Ltd.
Favorite Brand Name Recipes at www.fbnr.com

Pictured on the front cover *(clockwise from top left):* Lipton® Onion Burgers *(page 20),* Pizza Meat Loaf *(page 6),* Lasagna Supreme *(page 20)* and Fast 'n' Easy Chili *(page 78).*

Pictured on the back cover: Campbell's® Country Skillet Supper *(page 48).*

ISBN: 0-7853-5493-X

Manufactured in China.

8 7 6 5 4 3 2 1

Microwave Cooking: Microwave ovens vary in wattage. Use the cooking times as guidelines and check for doneness before adding more time.

Preparation/Cooking Times: Preparation times are based on the approximate amount of time required to assemble the recipe before cooking, baking, chilling or serving. These times include preparation steps such as measuring, chopping and mixing. The fact that some preparations and cooking can be done simultaneously is taken into account. Preparation of optional ingredients and serving suggestions is not included.

CONTENTS

★★★

ENCHANTING CLASSICS

6

HOCUS-POCUS CASSEROLES

24

MAGICAL SKILLET DISHES

42

PRESTO SOUPS, STEWS & CHILI

58

IN A FLASH

74

ACKNOWLEDGMENTS

91

INDEX

92

ENCHANTING CLASSICS

★★★

PIZZA MEAT LOAF

1 envelope LIPTON® RECIPE SECRETS® Onion Soup Mix*
2 pounds ground beef
1½ cups fresh bread crumbs
2 eggs
1 small green bell pepper, chopped (optional)
¼ cup water
1 cup RAGÚ® OLD WORLD STYLE® Pasta Sauce
1 cup shredded mozzarella cheese (about 4 ounces)

*Also terrific with LIPTON® RECIPE SECRETS® Savory Herb with Garlic Soup Mix.

1. Preheat oven to 350°F. In large bowl, combine all ingredients except ½ cup pasta sauce and ½ cup cheese.

2. In 13×9-inch baking or roasting pan, shape into loaf. Top with remaining ½ cup pasta sauce.

3. Bake uncovered 50 minutes.

4. Sprinkle top with remaining ½ cup cheese. Bake an additional 10 minutes or until done. Let stand 10 minutes before serving. *Makes 8 servings*

MAGIC TIP

When grating cheese, spray your box grater with nonstick cooking spray and place on a sheet of waxed paper. When you finish grating, clean-up is a breeze. Simply discard the waxed paper and rinse the grater clean.

CAMPBELL'S® FIESTA TACO SALAD

1 pound ground beef
2 tablespoons chili powder
1 can (10¾ ounces) CAMPBELL'S®
  Condensed Tomato Soup
8 cups salad greens, torn into bite-size
  pieces
2 cups tortilla chips
  Chopped tomato
  Sliced green onions
  Shredded Cheddar cheese
  Sliced pitted ripe olives

1. In medium skillet over medium-high heat, cook beef and chili powder until beef is browned, stirring to separate meat. Pour off fat.

2. Add soup. Reduce heat to low and heat through.

3. Arrange salad greens and chips on platter. Spoon meat mixture over salad greens. Top with tomato, onions, cheese and olives.

Makes 4 servings

Prep Time: 10 minutes
Cook Time: 15 minutes

EASY MOSTACCIOLI CASSEROLE

1 pound ground beef
½ onion, chopped
1 can (14½ ounces) tomatoes, chopped and
  undrained
1 can (8 ounces) tomato sauce
1 cup chopped olives
¼ cup Parmesan cheese
2 teaspoons LAWRY'S® Garlic Pepper
¼ teaspoons LAWRY'S® Seasoned Salt
½ teaspoon oregano
8 ounces Mostaccioli noodles, cooked and
  drained
1 cup (8 ounces) grated Mozzarella cheese

In large skillet, brown ground beef until crumbly; drain fat. Add onion, tomatoes, tomato sauce, olives, Parmesan cheese, Garlic Pepper, Seasoned Salt and oregano. Bring to a boil over medium-high heat; reduce heat to low and simmer, uncovered, 20 minutes. In 2-quart ovenproof casserole dish, place hot pasta, cover with meat mixture and top with cheese. Heat under broiler 3 minutes.   *Makes 8 servings*

Serving Suggestion: Serve with tossed green salad and herbed French bread.

MAGIC TIP ....

Save time by using packaged pre-shredded Cheddar cheese and checking the salad bar at your supermarket for pre-cut greens, toppers and trimmings.

....

Campbell's® Fiesta Taco Salad

DEEP DISH ALL-AMERICAN PIZZA

SAUCE
  1 pound lean ground beef
  ½ cup chopped onion
  ½ cup chopped green pepper
  1 cup ketchup
  1 tablespoon Worcestershire sauce
  1 teaspoon dry mustard
  1 teaspoon garlic salt
  ¼ teaspoon black pepper

CRUST
  3 to 3½ cups all-purpose flour, divided
  1 package RED STAR® Active Dry Yeast or QUICK•RISE™ Yeast
  1½ teaspoons salt
  1 cup warm water
  3 tablespoons oil

TOPPINGS
  2 medium firm, ripe tomatoes, sliced
  1 cup sliced fresh mushrooms
  2 cups (8 ounces) shredded Cheddar cheese

Preheat oven to 425°F.

Cook and stir beef, onion and green pepper in skillet until meat is lightly browned; drain if necessary. Add ketchup, Worcestershire sauce, mustard, garlic salt and black pepper. Simmer 15 minutes.

In large mixer bowl, combine 1½ cups flour, yeast and salt; mix well. Add very warm water (120° to 130°F) and oil to flour mixture. Blend at low speed until moistened; beat 3 minutes at medium speed. Gradually stir in enough remaining flour to make a firm dough. Knead 3 to 5 minutes on floured surface and roll dough into 16-inch circle or 15×11-inch rectangle. Place in greased 14-inch round deep-dish pizza pan or 13×9-inch baking pan, pushing dough halfway up sides of pan. Cover; let rise in warm place about 15 minutes.

Spread sauce over dough. Arrange tomatoes on sauce. Sprinkle mushrooms on top. Sprinkle with cheese. Bake 20 to 25 minutes or until edge is crisp and golden brown and cheese is melted. Serve immediately.

Makes one 14-inch round or 13×9-inch deep-dish pizza

Tip: Pizza may also be baked in a lasagna pan.

CAMPBELL'S® QUICK BEEF 'N' BEANS TACOS

  1 pound ground beef
  1 small onion, chopped (about ¼ cup)
  1 can (11¼ ounces) CAMPBELL'S® Condensed Fiesta Chili Beef Soup
  ¼ cup water
  10 taco shells
    Shredded Cheddar cheese, shredded lettuce, diced tomato and sour cream

1. In medium skillet over medium-high heat, cook beef and onion until beef is browned, stirring to separate meat. Pour off fat.

2. Add soup and water. Reduce heat to low. Cover and cook 5 minutes.

3. Divide meat mixture among taco shells. Top with cheese, lettuce, tomato and sour cream.

Makes 10 tacos

Prep Time: 15 minutes
Cook Time: 10 minutes

SPECIAL OCCASION MEAT LOAF

1 pound ground beef
1 pound Italian sausage, removed from casings and crumbled
1½ cups seasoned bread crumbs
2 eggs, lightly beaten
2 tablespoons chopped fresh parsley
2 cloves garlic, minced
1 teaspoon salt
½ teaspoon pepper
2 cups water
1 tablespoon butter
1 package (about 4 ounces) Spanich rice mix
2 packages (10 ounces each) frozen chopped spinach, thawed and well drained

Combine ground beef, sausage, bread crumbs, eggs, parsley, garlic, salt and pepper in large bowl; mix well. Place on 12×12-inch sheet of aluminum foil moistened with water. Cover with 12×14-inch sheet of waxed paper moistened with water. Press meat mixture into 12×12-inch rectangle with hands or rolling pin. Refrigerate 2 hours or until well chilled.

Bring water, butter and rice mix to a boil in medium saucepan. Continue boiling over medium heat 10 minutes or until rice is tender, stirring occasionally. Refrigerate 2 hours or until well chilled.

Preheat oven to 350°F. Remove waxed paper from ground beef mixture. Spread spinach over ground beef mixture, leaving 1-inch border. Spread rice evenly over spinach. Starting at long end, roll up jelly-roll style, using foil as a guide and removing foil after rolling. Seal edges tightly. Place meat loaf seam-side down in 13×9-inch baking pan. Bake, uncovered, about 1 hour. Let stand 15 minutes before serving. Cut into 1-inch slices.

Makes about 8 servings

MANICOTTI PARMIGIANA

1 package (1.5 ounces) LAWRY'S® Original Style Spaghetti Sauce Spices & Seasonings
1 can (1 pound 12 ounces) whole tomatoes, cut up
1 can (8 ounces) tomato sauce
2 tablespoons LAWRY'S® Garlic Spread Concentrate
12 manicotti shells
1 pound ground beef
¼ cup chopped green bell pepper
½ pound mozzarella cheese, grated
Grated Parmesan cheese
Finely chopped parsley (garnish)

In large saucepan, combine the first 4 ingredients. Bring to a boil over medium-high heat; reduce heat to low, cover and simmer 20 minutes, stirring occasionally. Meanwhile, cook manicotti shells according to package directions (about 7 minutes); drain. In medium skillet, brown ground beef and green pepper until beef is crumbly; drain fat. Remove from heat and add mozzarella cheese. Stuff manicotti shells with meat-cheese mixture. Pour ¾ of spaghetti sauce mixture into the bottom of 13×9×2-inch baking dish. Place stuffed manicotti shells over sauce mixture; top with remaining sauce. Sprinkle with Parmesan cheese. Bake, uncovered, in 375°F. oven 30 minutes. *Makes about 8 servings*

Serving Suggestion: Garnish with chopped parsley.

POLYNESIAN BURGERS

¼ cup LAWRY'S® Teriyaki Marinade with
    Pineapple Juice
1 pound ground beef
½ cup chopped green bell pepper
4 onion-flavored hamburger buns
1 can (5¼ ounces) pineapple slices,
    drained
    Lettuce leaves

In medium bowl, combine Teriyaki Marinade, ground beef and bell pepper; mix well. Let stand 10 to 15 minutes. Shape into 4 patties. Grill or broil burgers 8 to 10 minutes or until desired doneness, turning halfway through grilling time. Serve burgers on onion buns topped with pineapple slices and lettuce.

Makes 4 servings

Serving Suggestion: Serve with assorted fresh fruits.

Hint: For extra teriyaki flavor, brush buns and pineapple slices with additional Teriyaki Marinade; grill or broil until buns are lightly toasted and pineapple is heated through.

SLOPPY ONION JOES

1½ pounds ground beef
1 envelope LIPTON® RECIPE SECRETS®
    Onion Soup Mix
1 cup water
1 cup ketchup
2 tablespoons firmly packed brown sugar

1. In 10-inch skillet, brown ground beef over medium-high heat; drain.

2. Stir in remaining ingredients. Bring to a boil over high heat.

3. Reduce heat to low and simmer uncovered, stirring occasionally, 8 minutes or until mixture thickens. Serve, if desired, on hoagie rolls or hamburger buns. *Makes 6 servings*

FOUR-CHEESE LASAGNA

½ pound ground beef
½ cup chopped onion
⅓ cup chopped celery
1 clove garlic, minced
1½ teaspoons dried basil leaves
¼ teaspoon dried oregano leaves
¼ teaspoon salt
⅛ teaspoon ground black pepper
1 package (3 ounces) cream cheese, cubed
⅓ cup light cream or milk
½ cup dry white wine
½ cup (2 ounces) shredded Wisconsin
    Cheddar or Gouda cheese
1 egg, slightly beaten
1 cup cream-style cottage cheese
6 ounces lasagna noodles, cooked and
    drained
6 ounces sliced Wisconsin Mozzarella
    cheese

In large skillet, brown meat with onion, celery and garlic; drain. Stir in basil, oregano, salt and pepper. Reduce heat to low. Add cream cheese and cream. Cook, stirring frequently, until cream cheese is melted. Stir in wine. Gradually add Cheddar cheese, stirring until Cheddar cheese is almost melted. Remove from heat. In small bowl, combine egg and cottage cheese.

Into greased 10×6-inch baking dish, layer ½ each of the noodles, meat sauce, cottage cheese mixture and Mozzarella cheese; repeat layers. Bake, uncovered, at 375°F, 30 to 35 minutes or until hot and bubbly. Let stand 10 minutes before cutting to serve.

Makes 6 servings

Prep Time: 1½ hours
*Favorite recipe from **Wisconsin Milk Marketing Board***

Polynesian Burger

PREGO® BAKED ZITI SUPREME

1 pound ground beef
1 medium onion, chopped (about ½ cup)
1 jar (28 ounces) PREGO® Pasta Sauce
    with Fresh Mushrooms
1½ cups shredded mozzarella cheese
    (6 ounces)
5 cups hot cooked medium tube-shaped
    macaroni (about 3 cups uncooked)
¼ cup grated Parmesan cheese

1. In large saucepan over medium-high heat, cook beef and onion until beef is browned, stirring to separate meat. Pour off fat.

2. Stir in pasta sauce, *1 cup* mozzarella cheese and macaroni. Spoon into 3-quart shallow baking dish. Sprinkle with remaining mozzarella cheese and Parmesan cheese. Bake at 350°F. for 30 minutes.   *Makes 6 servings*

Tip: A salad of mixed greens and hot toasted garlic bread team perfectly with this quick and easy casserole.

Prep Time: 25 minutes
Cook Time: 30 minutes

MEDITERRANEAN BURGERS

½ cup feta cheese (2 ounces)
¼ cup A.1.® Original or A.1.® BOLD &
    SPICY Steak Sauce, divided
2 tablespoons sliced pitted ripe olives
2 tablespoons mayonnaise
1 pound ground beef
4 (5-inch) pita breads
4 radicchio leaves
4 tomato slices

Mix feta cheese, 2 tablespoons steak sauce, olives and mayonnaise. Cover; refrigerate at least one hour or up to 2 days.

Shape beef into 4 patties. Grill burgers over medium heat or broil 6 inches from heat source 5 minutes on each side or until no longer pink in center, basting with remaining 2 tablespoons steak sauce.

Split open top edge of each pita bread. Arrange 1 radicchio leaf in each pita pocket; top each with burger, tomato slice and 2 tablespoons chilled sauce. Serve immediately.

Makes 4 servings

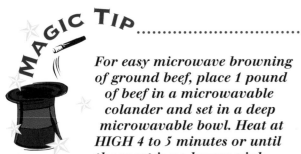

MAGIC TIP ....

For easy microwave browning of ground beef, place 1 pound of beef in a microwavable colander and set in a deep microwavable bowl. Heat at HIGH 4 to 5 minutes or until the meat is no longer pink, stirring twice during cooking. Discard the grease which accumulates in the bowl.

Prego® Baked Ziti Supreme

SOUTHWESTERN MEAT LOAF

1 envelope LIPTON® RECIPE SECRETS®
    Onion Soup Mix*
2 pounds ground beef
2 cups (about 3 ounces) cornflakes or bran
    flakes cereal, crushed
1½ cups frozen or drained canned whole
    kernel corn
1 small green bell pepper, chopped
2 eggs
¾ cup water
⅓ cup ketchup

*Also terrific with LIPTON® RECIPE SECRETS® Onion-
Mushroom or Beefy Onion Soup Mix.*

1. Preheat oven to 350°F. In large bowl,
combine all ingredients.

2. In 13×9-inch baking or roasting pan, shape
into loaf.

3. Bake uncovered 1 hour or until done. Let
stand 10 minutes before serving. Serve, if
desired, with salsa.   *Makes 8 servings*

PREGO® EASY SPAGHETTI & MEATBALLS

1 pound ground beef
2 tablespoons water
⅓ cup seasoned dry bread crumbs
1 egg, beaten
1 jar (28 ounces) PREGO® Traditional
    Pasta Sauce *or* Pasta Sauce Flavored
    with Meat
4 cups hot cooked spaghetti

1. Mix beef, water, bread crumbs and egg.
Shape meat mixture into 12 (2-inch) meatballs.
Arrange in 2-quart shallow microwave-safe
baking dish.

2. Microwave on HIGH 5 minutes or until
meatballs are no longer pink in center (160°F).
Pour off fat. Pour pasta sauce over meatballs.
Cover and microwave 3 minutes more or until
sauce is hot. Serve over spaghetti.
    Makes 4 servings

Prep Time: 15 minutes
Cook Time: 10 minutes

MAGIC TIP ....

*For a great lunchbox treat,
wrap leftover meat loaf slices
in a tortilla and top with
your favorite taco toppings
such as salsa, sour cream,
grated cheese and shredded
lettuce.*

....

Southwestern Meat Loaf

CONTADINA® CLASSIC LASAGNE

1 pound dry lasagne noodles, cooked
1 tablespoon olive or vegetable oil
1 cup chopped onion
½ cup chopped green bell pepper
2 cloves garlic, minced
1½ pounds lean ground beef
2 cans (14.5 ounces each) CONTADINA® Recipe Ready Diced Tomatoes, undrained
1 can (8 ounces) CONTADINA® Tomato Sauce
1 can (6 ounces) CONTADINA® Tomato Paste
½ cup dry red wine or beef broth
1½ teaspoons salt
1 teaspoon dried oregano leaves, crushed
1 teaspoon dried basil leaves, crushed
½ teaspoon ground black pepper
1 egg
1 cup (8 ounces) ricotta cheese
2 cups (8 ounces) shredded mozzarella cheese, divided

1. Cook pasta according to package directions; drain.

2. Meanwhile, heat oil in large skillet. Add onion, bell pepper and garlic; sauté for 3 minutes or until vegetables are tender.

3. Add beef; cook for 5 to 6 minutes or until evenly browned.

4. Add tomatoes and juice, tomato sauce, tomato paste, wine, salt, oregano, basil and black pepper; bring to a boil. Reduce heat to low; simmer, uncovered, for 20 minutes, stirring occasionally.

5. Beat egg slightly in medium bowl. Stir in ricotta cheese and 1 cup mozzarella cheese.

6. Layer noodles, half of meat sauce, noodles, all of ricotta cheese mixture, noodles and remaining meat sauce in ungreased 13×9-inch baking dish. Sprinkle with remaining mozzarella cheese.

7. Bake in preheated 350°F oven for 25 to 30 minutes or until heated through. Let stand for 10 minutes before cutting to serve.
Makes 10 servings

Prep Time: 35 minutes
Cook Time: 30 minutes
Standing Time: 10 minutes

TEMPTING TACO BURGERS

1 envelope LIPTON® RECIPE SECRETS® Onion-Mushroom Soup Mix*
1 pound ground beef
½ cup chopped tomato
¼ cup finely chopped green bell pepper
1 teaspoon chili powder
¼ cup water

Also terrific with LIPTON® RECIPE SECRETS® Onion, Garlic Mushroom, Beefy Onion or Beefy Mushroom Soup Mix.

1. In large bowl, combine all ingredients; shape into 4 patties.

2. Grill or broil until done. Serve, if desired, on hamburger buns and top with shredded lettuce and Cheddar cheese. *Makes 4 servings*

Recipe Tip: The best way to test for doneness of beef, pork, fish and poultry is to use a meat thermometer or an instant read thermometer, inserted into the thickest part of the meat.

SAUCY STUFFED PEPPERS

6 medium green bell peppers
1¼ cups water
2 cups low-sodium tomato juice, divided
1 can (6 ounces) tomato paste
1 teaspoon dried oregano leaves, crushed, divided
½ teaspoon dried basil leaves, crushed
½ teaspoon garlic powder, divided
1 pound lean ground beef
1½ cups QUAKER® Oats (quick or old fashioned, uncooked)
1 medium tomato, chopped
¼ cup chopped carrot
¼ cup chopped onion

Heat oven to 350°F. Cut peppers in half lengthwise. Remove membranes and seeds; set peppers aside. In large saucepan, combine water, 1 cup tomato juice, tomato paste, ½ teaspoon oregano, basil and ¼ teaspoon garlic powder. Simmer 10 to 15 minutes.

Combine beef, oats, remaining 1 cup tomato juice, ½ teaspoon oregano and ¼ teaspoon garlic powder with tomato, carrot and onion; mix well. Fill each pepper half with about ⅓ cup meat mixture. Place in 13×9-inch glass baking dish; pour sauce evenly over peppers. Bake 45 to 50 minutes.   *Makes 12 servings*

MINI MEAT LOAVES & VEGETABLES

1½ pounds lean ground beef
1 egg
1 can (8 ounces) tomato sauce, divided
1⅓ cups *French's® Taste Toppers™* French Fried Onions, divided
½ teaspoon salt
½ teaspoon Italian seasoning
6 small red potatoes, thinly sliced (about 1½ cups)
1 bag (16 ounces) frozen vegetable combination (broccoli, corn, red pepper), thawed and drained
Salt
Black pepper

Preheat oven to 375°F. In medium bowl, combine ground beef, egg, *½ can* tomato sauce, *⅔ cup Taste Toppers*, ½ teaspoon salt and Italian seasoning. Shape into 3 mini loaves and place in 9×13-inch baking dish. Arrange potatoes around loaves. Bake, covered, at 375°F for 35 minutes. Spoon vegetables around meat loaves; stir to combine with potatoes. Lightly season vegetables with salt and pepper, if desired. Top meat loaves with remaining tomato sauce. Bake, uncovered, 15 minutes or until meat loaves are done. Top loaves with remaining *⅔ cup Taste Toppers*; bake, uncovered, 5 minutes or until *Taste Toppers* are golden brown.   *Makes 6 servings*

Microwave Directions: Prepare meat loaves as directed above. Arrange potatoes on bottom of 8×12-inch microwave-safe dish; place meat loaves on potatoes. Cook, covered, on HIGH 13 minutes. Rotate dish halfway through cooking time. Add vegetables and season as above. Top meat loaves with remaining tomato sauce. Cook, covered, 7 minutes or until meat loaves are done. Rotate dish halfway through cooking time. Top loaves with remaining *⅔ cup* onions; cook, uncovered, 1 minute. Let stand 5 minutes.

LASAGNA SUPREME

8 ounces lasagna noodles
½ pound ground beef
½ pound mild Italian sausage, casings removed
1 medium onion, chopped
2 cloves garlic, minced
1 can (14½ ounces) whole peeled tomatoes, undrained and chopped
1 can (6 ounces) tomato paste
2 teaspoons dried basil leaves
1 teaspoon dried marjoram leaves
1 can (4 ounces) sliced mushrooms, drained
2 eggs
1 pound cream-style cottage cheese
¾ cup grated Parmesan cheese, divided
2 tablespoons dried parsley flakes
½ teaspoon salt
½ teaspoon black pepper
2 cups (8 ounces) shredded Cheddar cheese
3 cups (12 ounces) shredded mozzarella cheese

1. Cook lasagna noodles according to package directions; drain.

2. Cook meats, onion and garlic in large skillet over medium-high heat until meat is brown, stirring to separate meat. Drain.

3. Add tomatoes with juice, tomato paste, basil and marjoram. Reduce heat to low. Cover; simmer 15 minutes, stirring often. Stir in mushrooms; set aside.

4. Preheat oven to 375°F. Beat eggs in large bowl; add cottage cheese, ½ cup Parmesan cheese, parsley, salt and pepper. Mix well.

5. Place half the noodles into the bottom of 13×9-inch baking pan. Spread half the cottage cheese mixture over noodles, then half the meat mixture and half the Cheddar cheese and mozzarella cheese. Repeat layers. Sprinkle with remaining ¼ cup Parmesan cheese.

6. Bake lasagna 40 to 45 minutes or until bubbly. Let stand 10 minutes before cutting.

Makes 8 to 10 servings

Note: Lasagna may be assembled, covered and refrigerated up to 2 days in advance. Bake, uncovered, in preheated 375°F oven 60 minutes or until bubbly.

LIPTON® ONION BURGERS

2 pounds ground beef
1 envelope LIPTON® RECIPE SECRETS® Onion Soup Mix*
½ cup water

Also terrific with LIPTON® RECIPE SECRETS® Beefy Onion, Onion-Mushroom, Beefy Mushroom or Savory Herb with Garlic, or Garlic Mushroom Soup Mix.

1. In large bowl, combine all ingredients; shape into 8 patties.

2. Grill or broil to desired doneness.

Makes about 8 servings

MAGIC TIP

Use the direct cooking method for quick-cooking foods such as hamburgers. For this method, arrange the coals in a single layer directly under the food.

Lasagna Supreme

GRILLED MEAT LOAVES AND POTATOES

1 pound ground beef
½ cup A.1.® Original or A.1.® BOLD &
    SPICY Steak Sauce, divided
½ cup plain dry bread crumbs
1 egg, beaten
¼ cup finely chopped green bell pepper
¼ cup finely chopped onion
2 tablespoons margarine or butter, melted
4 (6-ounce) red skin potatoes, blanched,
    sliced into ¼-inch-thick rounds
    Grated Parmesan cheese
    Additional A.1.® Original or A.1.® BOLD
    & SPICY Steak Sauce (optional)

Mix ground beef, ¼ cup steak sauce, bread crumbs, egg, pepper and onion. Shape mixture into 4 (4-inch) oval-shaped loaves; set aside.

Blend remaining ¼ cup steak sauce and margarine; set aside.

Grill meat loaves over medium heat 20 to 25 minutes and potato slices 10 to 12 minutes or until beef is no longer pink in center and potatoes are tender, turning and basting both occasionally with reserved steak sauce mixture. Sprinkle cheese on potatoes. Serve immediately with additional steak sauce if desired.

Makes 4 servings

LASAGNA ROLL-UPS

1 pound ground beef
1 (16-ounce) jar spaghetti sauce
¼ cup A.1.® Steak Sauce
½ teaspoon dried basil leaves
1 (15-ounce) container ricotta cheese
1 egg, beaten
¼ cup grated Parmesan cheese, divided
8 lasagna noodles, cooked
2 cups shredded mozzarella cheese
    (8 ounces)

Brown ground beef in skillet over medium-high heat, stirring occasionally to break up meat; drain. In small bowl, mix spaghetti sauce, steak sauce and basil; stir half the sauce mixture into beef. In another bowl, mix ricotta cheese, egg and 2 tablespoons Parmesan cheese.

On each lasagna noodle, spread about ¼ cup ricotta mixture. Top with about ⅓ cup beef mixture and ¼ cup mozzarella cheese. Roll up each noodle from short end; stand on end in greased 2-quart casserole. Pour remaining sauce over noodles. Sprinkle with remaining Parmesan cheese.

Bake at 350°F for 45 minutes or until hot and bubbly. Serve with additional Parmesan cheese if desired. *Makes 4 to 6 servings*

Microwave Directions: In 2-quart microwave-safe casserole, crumble beef; cover. Microwave at HIGH (100% power) for 5 to 6 minutes or until browned; drain. Mix spaghetti sauce, steak sauce and basil; stir half the sauce mixture into beef. Fill lasagna rolls as above; arrange in same 2-quart casserole. Top with remaining sauce and parmesan cheese; cover. Microwave at HIGH for 10 to 12 minutes or until hot and bubbly, rotating dish ½ turn after 5 minutes. Let stand 3 minutes before serving.

Grilled Meat Loaf and Potatoes

HOCUS-POCUS CASSEROLES

★★★

BEEFY NACHO CRESCENT BAKE

    1 pound lean ground beef
    ½ cup chopped onion
    ¼ teaspoon salt
    ⅛ teaspoon black pepper
    1 tablespoon chili powder
    1 teaspoon ground cumin
    1 teaspoon dried oregano leaves
    1 can (11 ounces) condensed nacho cheese soup, undiluted
    1 cup milk
    1 can (8 ounces) refrigerated crescent roll dough
    ¼ cup (1 ounce) shredded Cheddar cheese
      Chopped fresh cilantro (optional)
      Salsa (optional)

PREHEAT oven to 375°F. Spray 13×9-inch baking dish with nonstick cooking spray. Place beef and onion in large skillet; season with salt and pepper. Brown beef over medium-high heat until no longer pink, stirring to separate meat. Drain fat. Stir in chili powder, cumin and oregano. Cook and stir 2 minutes; remove from heat.

COMBINE soup and milk in medium bowl, stirring until smooth. Pour soup mixture into prepared dish, spreading evenly.

SEPARATE crescent dough into 4 rectangles; press perforations together firmly. Roll each rectangle to 8×4 inches. (Sprinkle with flour to minimize sticking, if necessary.) Cut each rectangle in half crosswise to form 8 (4-inch) squares.

SPOON about ¼ cup beef mixture in center of each square. Lift 4 corners of dough up over filling to meet in center; pinch and twist firmly to seal. Place squares in dish.

BAKE, uncovered, 20 to 25 minutes or until crusts are golden brown. Sprinkle cheese over squares. Bake 5 minutes or until cheese melts. To serve, spoon soup mixture in dish over each serving; sprinkle with cilantro, if desired. Serve with salsa, if desired. *Makes 4 servings*

BEEF STROGANOFF CASSEROLE

1 pound lean ground beef
¼ teaspoon salt
⅛ teaspoon black pepper
1 teaspoon vegetable oil
8 ounces sliced mushrooms
1 large onion, chopped
3 cloves garlic, minced
¼ cup dry white wine
1 can (10¾ ounces) condensed cream of
   mushroom soup, undiluted
½ cup sour cream
1 tablespoon Dijon mustard
4 cups cooked egg noodles
   Chopped fresh parsley (optional)

Preheat oven to 350°F. Spray 13×9-inch baking dish with nonstick cooking spray.

Place beef in large skillet; season with salt and pepper. Brown beef over medium-high heat until no longer pink, stirring to separate beef. Drain fat from skillet; set beef aside.

Heat oil in same skillet over medium-high heat until hot. Add mushrooms, onion and garlic; cook 2 minutes or until onion is tender, stirring often. Add wine; reduce heat to medium-low and simmer 3 minutes. Remove from heat; stir in soup, sour cream and mustard until well combined. Return beef to skillet.

Place noodles in prepared dish. Pour beef mixture over noodles; stir until noodles are well coated.

Bake, uncovered, 30 minutes or until heated through. Sprinkle with parsley, if desired.

Makes 6 servings

CALIFORNIA TAMALE PIE

1 pound ground beef
1 cup yellow corn meal
2 cups milk
2 eggs, beaten
1 package (1.48 ounces) LAWRY'S® Spices
   & Seasonings for Chili
2 teaspoons LAWRY'S® Seasoned Salt
1 can (17 ounces) whole kernel corn,
   drained
1 can (14½ ounces) whole tomatoes, cut
   up
1 can (2¼ ounces) sliced ripe olives,
   drained
1 cup (4 ounces) shredded cheddar cheese

In medium skillet, cook ground beef until browned and crumbly; drain fat. In 2½-quart casserole dish, combine corn meal, milk and egg; mix well. Add ground beef and remaining ingredients except cheese; stir to mix. Bake, uncovered, in 350°F oven 1 hour and 15 minutes. Add cheese and continue baking until cheese melts. Let stand 10 minutes before serving.

Microwave Directions: In 2½-quart glass casserole, microwave ground beef on HIGH 5 to 6 minutes; drain fat and crumble beef. Mix in corn meal, milk and egg; blend well. Add remaining ingredients except cheese. Cover with plastic wrap, venting one corner. Microwave on HIGH 15 minutes, stirring after 8 minutes. Sprinkle cheese over top and microwave on HIGH 2 minutes. Let stand 10 minutes before serving.

Makes 6 to 8 servings

Serving Suggestion: Serve with mixed green salad flavored with kiwi and green onion.

Hint: Substitute 1 package (1.25 ounces) LAWRY'S® Taco Spices & Seasonings for Spices & Seasonings for Chili Seasoning Mix, if desired.

Beef Stroganoff Casserole

SPINACH-POTATO BAKE

1 pound extra-lean (90% lean) ground
　　beef
½ cup sliced fresh mushrooms
1 small onion, chopped
2 cloves garlic, minced
1 package (10 ounces) frozen chopped
　　spinach, thawed, well drained
½ teaspoon ground nutmeg
1 pound russet potatoes, peeled, cooked
　　and mashed
¼ cup light sour cream
¼ cup fat-free (skim) milk
　　Salt and black pepper
½ cup (2 ounces) shredded Cheddar cheese

Preheat oven to 400°F. Spray deep 9-inch
casserole dish with nonstick cooking spray.

Brown ground beef in large skillet. Drain. Add
mushrooms, onion and garlic; cook until
tender. Stir in spinach and nutmeg; cover. Heat
thoroughly, stirring occasionally.

Combine potatoes, sour cream and milk. Add to
ground beef mixture; season with salt and
pepper to taste. Spoon into prepared casserole
dish; sprinkle with cheese.

Bake 15 to 20 minutes or until slightly puffed
and cheese is melted. *Makes 6 servings*

MAGIC TIP

*USDA standards require that
all ground beef be at least
70 percent lean. Ground
sirloin and ground round are
the leanest. Ground chuck
contains more fat, so it
produces juicier hamburgers
and many other beef dishes.*

MALAYSIAN CURRIED BEEF

2 tablespoons vegetable oil
2 large yellow onions, chopped
1 piece fresh ginger (about 1 inch square),
　　minced
2 cloves garlic, minced
2 tablespoons curry powder
1 teaspoon salt
2 large baking potatoes (1 pound), peeled
　　and cut into chunks
1 cup beef broth
1 pound ground beef chuck
2 ripe tomatoes (12 ounces), peeled and
　　cut into chunks
　　Hot cooked rice
　　Purple kale and watercress sprigs for
　　garnish

1. Heat wok over medium-high heat 1 minute
or until hot. Drizzle oil into wok and heat
30 seconds. Add onions and stir-fry 2 minutes.
Add ginger, garlic, curry and salt to wok. Cook
and stir about 1 minute or until fragrant. Add
potatoes; cook and stir 2 to 3 minutes.

2. Add beef broth to potato mixture. Cover and
bring to a boil. Reduce heat to low; simmer
about 20 minutes or until potatoes are fork-
tender.

3. Stir ground beef into potato mixture. Cook
and stir about 5 minutes or until beef is
browned and no pink remains; spoon off fat if
necessary.

4. Add tomato chunks and stir gently until
thoroughly heated. Spoon beef mixture into
serving dish. Top center with rice. Garnish, if
desired. *Makes 4 servings*

PASTA "PIZZA"

3 eggs, slightly beaten
½ cup milk
2 cups corkscrew macaroni, cooked and
    drained
½ cup (2 ounces) shredded Wisconsin
    Cheddar cheese
¼ cup finely chopped onion
1 pound lean ground beef
1 can (15 ounces) tomato sauce
1 teaspoon dried basil leaves
1 teaspoon dried oregano leaves
½ teaspoon garlic salt
1 medium tomato, thinly sliced
1 green pepper, sliced into rings
1½ cups (6 ounces) shredded Wisconsin
    Mozzarella cheese

Combine eggs and milk in small bowl. Add to
hot macaroni; mix lightly to coat. Stir in
Cheddar cheese and onion; mix well. Spread
macaroni mixture onto bottom of well-buttered
14-inch pizza pan. Bake at 350°F for
25 minutes. Meanwhile, in large skillet over
medium-high heat, brown meat, stirring
occasionally to separate meat; drain. Stir in
tomato sauce, basil, oregano and garlic salt.
Spoon over macaroni crust. Arrange tomato
slices and pepper rings on top. Sprinkle with
Mozzarella cheese. Continue baking 15 minutes
or until cheese is bubbly.   *Makes 8 servings*

Prep time: 50 minutes

*Favorite recipe from **Wisconsin Milk Marketing Board***

ZUCCHINI LASAGNE

3 cans (8 ounces each) CONTADINA®
    Tomato Sauce
1 can (14.5 ounces) CONTADINA® Stewed
    Tomatoes, undrained
1 teaspoon granulated sugar
1 teaspoon Italian herb seasoning
1 teaspoon ground black pepper
1 pound lean ground beef
3 teaspoons seasoned salt
6 medium zucchini squash, sliced ⅛ inch
    thick
2 cups (8 ounces) shredded mozzarella
    cheese
2 cups (15 ounces) ricotta cheese
3 tablespoons grated Parmesan cheese

1. Combine tomato sauce, stewed tomatoes,
sugar, Italian seasoning and pepper in medium
saucepan.

2. Simmer, uncovered, for 25 minutes, stirring
occasionally. In medium skillet, brown beef;
drain. Stir in seasoned salt and tomato sauce
mixture.

3. Butter bottom of 13×9-inch baking dish.
Layer half of zucchini slices on bottom of
baking dish; sprinkle lightly with salt. Spread
half of ground beef mixture over zucchini.
Sprinkle with mozzarella cheese and evenly
spread all the ricotta cheese. Top with
remaining zucchini slices; sprinkle lightly with
salt. Spread with remaining beef mixture.
Sprinkle Parmesan cheese on top.

4. Bake in preheated 350° F oven for
45 minutes.   *Makes 8 cups*

Prep Time: 20 minutes
Cook Time: 70 minutes

TACOS IN PASTA SHELLS

1 package (3 ounces) cream cheese with chives
18 jumbo pasta shells
1¼ pounds ground beef
1 teaspoon salt
1 teaspoon chili powder
2 tablespoons butter, melted
1 cup prepared taco sauce
1 cup (4 ounces) shredded Cheddar cheese
1 cup (4 ounces) shredded Monterey Jack cheese
1½ cups crushed tortilla chips
1 cup sour cream
3 green onions, chopped
Leaf lettuce, small pitted ripe olives and cherry tomatoes, for garnish

1. Cut cream cheese into ½-inch cubes. Let stand at room temperature until softened.

2. Cook pasta according to package directions. Place in colander and rinse under warm running water. Drain well. Return to saucepan.

3. Preheat oven to 350°F. Butter 13×9-inch baking pan.

4. Cook beef in large skillet over medium-high heat until brown, stirring to separate meat; drain drippings.

5. Reduce heat to medium-low. Add cream cheese, salt and chili powder; simmer 5 minutes.

6. Toss shells with butter. Fill shells with beef mixture using spoon. Arrange shells in prepared pan. Pour taco sauce over each shell. Cover with foil.

7. Bake 15 minutes. Uncover; top with Cheddar cheese, Monterey Jack cheese and chips. Bake 15 minutes more or until bubbly. Top with sour cream and onions. Garnish, if desired.

Makes 4 to 6 servings

ARTICHOKE CASSEROLE

¾ pound extra-lean (90% lean) ground beef
½ cup sliced mushrooms
¼ cup chopped onion
1 clove garlic, minced
1 can (14 ounces) artichoke hearts, drained, rinsed, chopped
½ cup dry bread crumbs
¼ cup (1 ounce) grated Parmesan cheese
2 tablespoons chopped fresh rosemary *or* 1 teaspoon dried rosemary
1½ teaspoons chopped fresh marjoram *or* ½ teaspoon dried marjoram leaves
Salt and black pepper
3 egg whites

Preheat oven to 400°F. Spray 1-quart casserole with nonstick cooking spray.

Brown ground beef in medium skillet. Drain. Add mushrooms, onion and garlic; cook until tender.

Combine ground beef mixture, artichokes, crumbs, cheese, rosemary and marjoram; mix lightly. Season with salt and pepper to taste.

Beat egg whites until stiff peaks form; fold into ground beef mixture. Spoon into prepared casserole.

Bake 20 minutes or until lightly browned around edges. *Makes 4 servings*

Tacos in Pasta Shells

SHEPHERD'S PIE

1⅓ cups instant mashed potato buds
1⅔ cups milk
2 tablespoons margarine or butter
1 teaspoon salt, divided
1 pound ground beef
¼ teaspoon black pepper
1 jar (12 ounces) beef gravy
1 package (10 ounces) frozen mixed
    vegetables, thawed and drained
¾ cup grated Parmesan cheese

1. Preheat broiler. Prepare 4 servings of mashed potatoes according to package directions using milk, margarine and ½ teaspoon salt.

2. While mashed potatoes are cooking, brown meat in medium broilerproof skillet over medium-high heat, stirring to separate meat. Drain drippings. Sprinkle meat with remaining ½ teaspoon salt and pepper. Add gravy and vegetables; mix well. Cook over medium-low heat 5 minutes or until hot.

3. Spoon prepared potatoes around outside edge of skillet, leaving 3-inch circle in center. Sprinkle cheese evenly over potatoes. Broil 4 to 5 inches from heat source 3 minutes or until cheese is golden brown and meat mixture is bubbly.   *Makes 4 servings*

Prep and Cook Time: 28 minutes

MAGIC TIP

Keep packages of raw meat away from other food items, especially from produce and unwrapped products. The meat's juices can drip and contaminate other foods.

CAMPBELL'S® BEEF & MOZZARELLA BAKE

1 pound ground beef
1 can (11⅛ ounces) CAMPBELL'S®
    Condensed Italian Tomato Soup
1 can (10¾ ounces) CAMPBELL'S®
    Condensed Cream of Mushroom Soup
1¼ cups water
1 teaspoon dried basil leaves, crushed
¼ teaspoon pepper
⅛ teaspoon garlic powder *or* 1 clove garlic,
    minced
1½ cups shredded mozzarella cheese
    (6 ounces)
4 cups hot cooked medium shell macaroni
    (about 3 cups uncooked)

1. In medium skillet over medium-high heat, cook beef until browned, stirring to separate meat. Pour off fat.

2. Add soups, water, basil, pepper, garlic powder, *1 cup* cheese and macaroni. Spoon into 2-quart shallow baking dish. Bake at 400°F. for 20 minutes or until hot.

3. Stir. Sprinkle remaining cheese over beef mixture. Bake 5 minutes more or until cheese is melted.   *Makes 6 servings*

Variation: Substitute 4 cups hot cooked elbow macaroni (about 2 cups uncooked) for shell macaroni.

Prep Time: 15 minutes
Cook Time: 25 minutes

Shepherd's Pie

STRING PIE

1 pound ground beef
½ cup chopped onion
¼ cup chopped green pepper
1 jar (15½ ounces) spaghetti sauce
8 ounces spaghetti, cooked and drained
⅓ cup grated Parmesan cheese
2 eggs, beaten
2 teaspoons butter
1 cup cottage cheese
½ cup (2 ounces) shredded mozzarella
  cheese

Preheat oven to 350°F. Cook beef, onion and green pepper in large skillet over medium-high heat until meat is browned. Drain fat. Stir in spaghetti sauce. Combine spaghetti, Parmesan cheese, eggs and butter in large bowl; mix well. Place in bottom of 13×9-inch baking pan. Spread cottage cheese over top; cover with sauce mixture. Sprinkle with mozzarella cheese. Bake until mixture is thoroughly heated and cheese is melted, about 20 minutes.

Makes 6 to 8 servings

Favorite recipe from **North Dakota Beef Commission**

RANCH LENTIL CASSEROLE

2 cups lentils, rinsed
4 cups water
1 pound lean ground beef
1 cup water
1 cup ketchup
1 envelope dry onion soup mix
1 teaspoon prepared mustard
1 teaspoon vinegar

Cook lentils in 4 cups water for 30 minutes. Drain. Brown ground beef. Combine lentils, beef, 1 cup water and remaining ingredients in baking dish. Bake at 400°F for 30 minutes.

Makes 8 servings

Note: Prepared recipe can be frozen.

Favorite recipe from **USA Dry Pea & Lentil Council**

MEXICAN STUFFED SHELLS

1 pound ground beef
1 jar (12 ounces) mild or medium picante
  sauce
½ cup water
1 can (8 ounces) tomato sauce
1 can (4 ounces) chopped green chilies,
  drained
1 cup (4 ounces) shredded Monterey Jack
  cheese, divided
1⅓ cups *French's®️ Taste Toppers™️* French
  Fried Onions
12 pasta stuffing shells, cooked in unsalted
  water and drained

Preheat oven to 350°F. In large skillet, brown ground beef; drain. In small bowl, combine picante sauce, water and tomato sauce. Stir ½ cup sauce mixture into beef along with chilies, ½ cup cheese and ⅔ cup *Taste Toppers*; mix well. Spread half the remaining sauce mixture in bottom of 10-inch round baking dish. Stuff cooked shells with beef mixture. Arrange shells in baking dish; top with remaining sauce. Bake, covered, at 350°F for 30 minutes or until heated through. Top with remaining ⅔ cup *Taste Toppers* and cheese; bake, uncovered, 5 minutes or until cheese is melted.

Makes 6 servings

Microwave Directions: Crumble ground beef into medium microwave-safe bowl. Cook, covered, on HIGH (100%) 4 to 6 minutes or until beef is cooked. Stir beef halfway through cooking time. Drain well. Prepare sauce mixture as above; spread ½ cup in 12×8-inch microwave-safe dish. Prepare beef mixture as above. Stuff cooked shells with beef mixture. Arrange shells in dish; top with remaining sauce. Cook, covered, 10 to 12 minutes or until heated through. Rotate dish halfway through cooking time. Top with remaining onions and cheese; cook, uncovered, 1 minute or until cheese is melted. Let stand 5 minutes.

String Pie

MOUSSAKA

1 large eggplant
2½ teaspoons salt, divided
2 large zucchini
2 large russet potatoes, peeled
½ to ¾ cup olive oil, divided
5 tablespoons butter or margarine, divided
1 large onion, chopped
1½ pounds ground beef or lamb
2 cloves garlic, minced
1 cup chopped tomatoes
½ cup dry red or white wine
¼ cup chopped fresh parsley
¼ teaspoon ground cinnamon
⅛ teaspoon black pepper
1 cup grated Parmesan cheese, divided
⅓ cup all-purpose flour
¼ teaspoon ground nutmeg
2 cups milk

Cut eggplant lengthwise into ½-inch-thick slices. Place in large colander set over bowl; sprinkle with 1 teaspoon salt. Drain 30 minutes. Cut zucchini lengthwise into ⅜-inch-thick slices. Cut potatoes lengthwise into ¼-inch-thick slices.

Heat ¼ cup oil in large skillet over medium heat until hot. Add potatoes in single layer. Cook 5 minutes per side or until tender and lightly browned. Remove potatoes from skillet; drain on paper towels. Add more oil to skillet, if needed. Cook zucchini 2 minutes per side or until tender. Drain on paper towels. Add more oil to skillet. Cook eggplant 5 minutes per side or until tender. Drain on paper towels. Drain oil from skillet; discard.

Melt 1 tablespoon butter in same skillet over medium heat. Add onion. Cook and stir 5 minutes or until cooked through. Add beef and garlic to skillet. Cook and stir 10 minutes or until meat is no longer pink. Pour off drippings. Stir in tomatoes, wine, parsley, 1 teaspoon salt, cinnamon and pepper. Bring to a boil over high heat. Reduce heat to low. Simmer 10 minutes or until liquid is evaporated.

Preheat oven to 325°F. Grease 13×9-inch baking dish. Arrange potatoes in bottom; sprinkle with ¼ cup cheese. Top with zucchini and ¼ cup cheese, then eggplant and ¼ cup cheese. Spoon meat mixture over top.

To prepare sauce, melt remaining 4 tablespoons butter in medium saucepan over low heat. Blend in flour, remaining ½ teaspoon salt and nutmeg with wire whisk. Cook 1 minute, whisking constantly. Gradually whisk in milk. Cook over medium heat, until mixture boils and thickens, whisking constantly. Pour sauce evenly over meat mixture in dish; sprinkle with remaining ¼ cup cheese. Bake 30 to 40 minutes or until hot and bubbly. Garnish as desired.

Makes 6 to 8 servings

MONTEREY BLACK BEAN TORTILLA SUPPER

1 pound ground beef, browned and drained
1½ cups bottled salsa
1 (15-ounce) can black beans, drained
4 (8-inch) flour tortillas
2 cups (8 ounces) shredded Wisconsin Monterey Jack cheese*

For authentic Mexican flavor, substitute 2 cups shredded Wisconsin Queso Blanco.

Heat oven to 400°F. Combine ground beef, salsa and beans. In lightly greased 2-quart round casserole, layer one tortilla, ⅔ cup meat mixture and ½ cup cheese. Repeat layers three times. Bake 30 minutes or until heated through.

Makes 5 to 6 servings

*Favorite recipe from **Wisconsin Milk Marketing Board***

STUFFED MEXICAN PIZZA PIE

1 pound ground beef
1 large onion, chopped
1 large green bell pepper, chopped
1½ cups UNCLE BEN'S® Instant Rice
2 cans (14½ ounces each) Mexican-style stewed tomatoes, undrained
⅔ cup water
2 cups (8 ounces) shredded Mexican-style seasoned Monterey Jack-Colby cheese blend, divided
1 container (10 ounces) refrigerated pizza crust dough

1. Preheat oven to 425°F. Spray 13×9-inch baking pan with cooking spray; set aside.

2. Spray large nonstick skillet with nonstick cooking spray; heat over high heat until hot. Add beef, onion and bell pepper; cook and stir 5 minutes or until meat is no longer pink.

3. Add rice, stewed tomatoes and water. Bring to a boil. Pour beef mixture into prepared baking pan. Sprinkle with 1¼ cups cheese and stir until blended.

4. Unroll pizza crust dough on work surface. Place dough in one even layer over mixture in baking pan. Cut 6 to 8 slits in dough with sharp knife. Bake 10 minutes or until crust is lightly browned. Sprinkle top of crust with remaining ¾ cup cheese; continue baking 4 minutes or until cheese is melted and crust is deep golden brown.

5. Let stand 5 minutes before cutting.

Makes 6 servings

BEEF & ZUCCHINI QUICHE

1 unbaked 9-inch pie shell
½ pound lean ground beef
1 medium zucchini, shredded
3 green onions, sliced
¼ cup sliced mushrooms
1 tablespoon all-purpose flour
3 eggs, beaten
1 cup milk
¾ cup (3 ounces) shredded Swiss cheese
1½ teaspoons chopped fresh thyme *or*
    ½ teaspoon dried thyme leaves
½ teaspoon salt
    Dash black pepper
    Dash ground red pepper

Preheat oven to 475°F.

Line pie shell with foil; fill with dried beans or rice. Bake 8 minutes. Remove from oven; carefully remove foil and beans. Return pie shell to oven. Continue baking 4 minutes; set aside. *Reduce oven temperature to 375°F.*

Brown ground beef in medium skillet. Drain. Add zucchini, onions and mushrooms; cook, stirring occasionally, until vegetables are tender. Stir in flour; cook 2 minutes, stirring constantly. Remove from heat.

Combine eggs, milk, cheese and seasonings in medium bowl. Stir into ground beef mixture; pour into crust.

Bake 35 minutes or until knife inserted near center comes out clean. *Makes 6 servings*

TAMALE PIE

1 tablespoon olive or vegetable oil
1 small onion, chopped
1 pound ground beef
1 envelope LIPTON® RECIPE SECRETS®
    Onion Soup Mix*
1 can (14½ ounces) stewed tomatoes,
    undrained
½ cup water
1 can (15 to 19 ounces) red kidney beans,
    rinsed and drained
1 package (8½ ounces) corn muffin mix

Also terrific with LIPTON® RECIPE SECRETS® Fiesta Herb with Red Pepper, Onion-Mushroom, Beefy Onion or Beefy Mushroom Soup Mix.

• Preheat oven to 400°F.

• In 12-inch skillet, heat oil over medium heat and cook onion, stirring occasionally, 3 minutes or until tender. Stir in ground beef and cook until browned.

• Stir in onion soup mix blended with tomatoes and water. Bring to a boil over high heat, stirring with spoon to crush tomatoes. Reduce heat to low and stir in beans. Simmer uncovered, stirring occasionally, 10 minutes. Turn into 2-quart casserole.

• Prepare corn muffin mix according to package directions. Spoon evenly over casserole.

• Bake uncovered 15 minutes or until corn topping is golden and filling is hot.

Makes about 6 servings

GREEK-STYLE LASAGNA

1 pound ground beef
1 cup chopped onion
1 clove garlic, crushed OR ¼ teaspoon
    LAWRY'S® Garlic Powder with Parsley
1 teaspoon LAWRY'S® Seasoned Salt
½ teaspoon LAWRY'S® Seasoned Pepper
1 package (1.5 ounces) LAWRY'S® Original
    Style Spaghetti Sauce Spices &
    Seasonings
1 can (6 ounces) tomato paste
2 cups water
¼ cup flour
½ teaspoon LAWRY'S® Seasoned Salt
1 eggplant
¾ cup salad oil
1 cup grated Parmesan cheese

In large skillet, cook ground beef until browned and crumbly; drain fat. Add onion, garlic, 1 teaspoon Seasoned Salt, Seasoned Pepper, Original Style Spaghetti Sauce Spice & Seasonings, tomato paste and water. Bring to a boil over medium-high heat, reduce heat to low, cover and simmer 15 minutes, stirring occasionally. Meanwhile, in small bowl, combine flour and ½ teaspoon Seasoned Salt. Peel eggplant and slice crosswise into ¼-inch thick slices. Place small amount of salad oil in medium skillet and heat. Lightly coat eggplant slices with seasoned flour. Quickly cook eggplant slices over medium-high heat, adding oil as necessary. (Use as little oil as possible.) Pour ¼ of meat sauce into a 12×8×2-inch baking dish. Cover meat sauce with ⅓ of eggplant slices. Sprinkle ¼ of Parmesan cheese over eggplant. Repeat layers 2 more times, ending with meat sauce and Parmesan cheese. Bake, uncovered, in 350 F. oven 30 minutes.

Makes 6 to 8 servings

Serving Suggestion: Serve with tossed green salad and fruit dessert.

Tamale Pie

LASAGNA BEEF 'N' SPINACH ROLL-UPS

1½ pounds ground beef
1 (28-ounce) jar spaghetti sauce
½ cup A.1.® Original or A.1.® BOLD &
    SPICY Steak Sauce
½ teaspoon dried basil leaves
1 (15-ounce) container ricotta cheese
1 (10-ounce) package frozen chopped
    spinach, thawed, well drained
2 cups shredded mozzarella cheese
    (8 ounces)
⅓ cup grated Parmesan cheese, divided
1 egg, beaten
12 lasagna noodles, cooked, drained
2 tablespoons chopped fresh parsley

In large skillet, over medium-high heat, brown beef until no longer pink, stirring occasionally to break up beef; drain. In small bowl, mix spaghetti sauce, steak sauce and basil; stir 1 cup spaghetti sauce mixture into beef. Set aside remaining sauce mixture.

In medium bowl, mix ricotta cheese, spinach, mozzarella cheese, 3 tablespoons Parmesan cheese and egg. On each lasagna noodle, spread about ¼ cup ricotta mixture. Top with about ⅓ cup beef mixture. Roll up each noodle from short end; lay each roll, seam side down, in lightly greased 13×9×2-inch baking dish. Pour reserved spaghetti sauce mixture over noodles. Sprinkle with remaining Parmesan cheese and parsley. Bake, covered, at 350°F 30 minutes. Uncover and bake 15 to 20 minutes more or until hot and bubbly. Serve with additional Parmesan cheese if desired. Garnish as desired. *Makes 6 servings*

HEARTLAND SHEPHERD'S PIE

¾ pound ground beef
1 medium onion, chopped
1 can (14½ ounces) DEL MONTE® Original
    Recipe Stewed Tomatoes
1 can (8 ounces) DEL MONTE® Tomato
    Sauce
1 can (14½ ounces) DEL MONTE® Mixed
    Vegetables, drained
  Instant mashed potato flakes plus
    ingredients to prepare (enough for
    6 servings)
3 cloves garlic, minced (optional)

1. Preheat oven to 375°F. In large skillet, brown meat and onion over medium-high heat; drain.

2. Add tomatoes and tomato sauce; cook over high heat until thickened, stirring frequently. Stir in mixed vegetables. Season with salt and pepper, if desired.

3. Spoon into 2-quart baking dish; set aside. Prepare 6 servings mashed potatoes according to package directions, first cooking garlic in specified amount of butter.

4. Top meat mixture with potatoes. Bake 20 minutes or until heated through. Garnish with chopped parsley, if desired.
Makes 4 to 6 servings

Prep Time: 5 minutes
Cook Time: 30 minutes

MAGIC TIP

Beef can fit into a healthy meal plan. It provides high-quality protein, including all eight essential amino acids; it is also an important source of dietary iron and zinc.

Lasagna Beef 'n' Spinach Roll-Ups

MAGICAL SKILLET DISHES

★★★

CHUCKWAGON BBQ RICE ROUND-UP

1 pound lean ground beef
1 (6.8-ounce) package RICE-A-RONI® Beef Flavor
2 tablespoons margarine or butter
2 cups frozen corn
½ cup prepared barbecue sauce
½ cup (2 ounces) shredded Cheddar cheese

1. In large skillet over medium-high heat, brown ground beef until well cooked. Remove from skillet; drain. Set aside.

2. In same skillet over medium heat, sauté rice-vermicelli mix with margarine until vermicelli is golden brown.

3. Slowly stir in 2½ cups water, corn and Special Seasonings; bring to a boil. Reduce heat to low. Cover; simmer 15 to 20 minutes or until rice is tender.

4. Stir in barbecue sauce and ground beef. Sprinkle with cheese. Cover; let stand 3 to 5 minutes or until cheese is melted.   *Makes 4 servings*

Prep Time: 5 minutes
Cook Time: 25 minutes

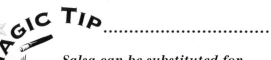

Salsa can be substituted for barbecue sauce.

RAGÚ® CHILI MAC

1 tablespoon olive or vegetable oil
1 medium green bell pepper, chopped
1 pound ground beef
1 jar (26 to 28 ounces) RAGÚ® Old World
 Style® Pasta Sauce
2 tablespoons chili powder
8 ounces elbow macaroni, cooked and
 drained

1. In 12-inch nonstick skillet, heat oil over medium-high heat and cook green bell pepper, stirring occasionally, 3 minutes. Add ground beef and brown, stirring occasionally; drain.

2. Stir in Ragú Pasta Sauce and chili powder. Bring to a boil over high heat. Reduce heat to low and simmer covered 10 minutes.

3. Stir in macaroni and heat through. Serve, if desired, with sour cream and shredded Cheddar cheese.   *Makes 4 servings*

Prep Time: 10 minutes
Cook Time: 25 minutes

JOE'S SPECIAL

1 pound lean ground beef
2 cups sliced mushrooms
1 small onion, chopped
2 teaspoons Worcestershire sauce
1 teaspoon dried oregano leaves
1 teaspoon ground nutmeg
½ teaspoon garlic powder
½ teaspoon salt
1 package (10 ounces) frozen chopped
 spinach, thawed
4 large eggs, lightly beaten
⅓ cup grated Parmesan cheese

1. Spray large skillet with nonstick cooking spray. Add ground beef, mushrooms and onion; cook over medium-high heat 6 to 8 minutes or until onion is tender, breaking beef apart with wooden spoon. Add Worcestershire, oregano, nutmeg, garlic powder and salt. Cook until meat is no longer pink.

2. Drain spinach (do not squeeze dry); stir into meat mixture. Push mixture to one side of pan. Reduce heat to medium. Pour eggs into other side of pan; cook, without stirring, 1 to 2 minutes or until set on bottom. Lift eggs to allow uncooked portion to flow underneath. Repeat until softly set. Gently stir into meat mixture and heat through. Stir in cheese.
          Makes 4 to 6 servings

Serving Suggestion: Serve with salsa and toast.

Prep and Cook Time: 20 minutes

Ragú® Chili Mac

ITALIAN BEEF BURRITO

1½ pounds ground beef
  2 medium onions, finely chopped
  2 medium red and/or green bell peppers,
     chopped
  1 jar (26 to 28 ounces) RAGÚ® Hearty
     Robusto!™ Pasta Sauce
  ½ teaspoon dried oregano leaves, crushed
  8 (10-inch) flour tortillas, warmed
  2 cups shredded mozzarella cheese (about
     8 ounces)

1. In 12-inch skillet, brown ground beef over medium-high heat.

2. Stir in onions and red bell peppers and cook, stirring occasionally, 5 minutes or until tender; drain. Stir in Ragú Pasta Sauce and oregano; heat through.

3. To serve, top each tortilla with ¼ cup cheese and 1 cup ground beef mixture; roll up and serve.   *Makes 8 servings*

Prep Time: 15 minutes
Cook Time: 15 minutes

GREEK BEEF & RICE

  1 bag SUCCESS® Rice
  1 pound lean ground beef
  2 medium zucchini, sliced
  ½ cup chopped onion
  1 medium clove garlic, minced
  1 can (14½ ounces) tomato sauce
  ¾ teaspoon dried basil leaves, crushed
  ¾ teaspoon salt
  ¼ teaspoon pepper

Prepare rice according to package directions.

Brown beef in large skillet, stirring occasionally to separate beef. Pour off all but 2 tablespoons drippings. Add zucchini, onion and garlic to skillet; cook and stir until crisp-tender. Add all remaining ingredients *except* rice; cover. Simmer 10 minutes, stirring occasionally. Add rice; heat thoroughly, stirring occasionally. Garnish, if desired.   *Makes 6 servings*

MAGIC TIP

Burritos are flour tortillas that are filled with ground beef or various other fillings, then rolled up or folded into small "packages" with a rectangular shape. Burritos are typically served without a sauce, but may be garnished with sour cream or salsa.

Italian Beef Burrito

CAMPBELL'S® COUNTRY SKILLET SUPPER

1 pound ground beef
1 medium onion, chopped (about ½ cup)
⅛ teaspoon garlic powder *or* 1 clove garlic, minced
1 can (10¾ ounces) CAMPBELL'S® Condensed Golden Mushroom Soup
1 can (10½ ounces) CAMPBELL'S® Condensed Beef Broth
1 can (14½ ounces) diced tomatoes
1 small zucchini, sliced (about 1 cup)
½ teaspoon dried thyme leaves, crushed
1½ cups *uncooked* corkscrew pasta

1. In medium skillet over medium-high heat, cook beef, onion and garlic powder until beef is browned, stirring to separate meat. Pour off fat.

2. Add soup, broth, tomatoes, zucchini and thyme. Heat to a boil. Stir in pasta. Reduce heat to low. Cook 15 minutes or until pasta is done, stirring often. *Makes 4 servings*

Campbell's® Country Skillet Supper Provençal: Top with sliced pitted ripe olives.

Prep Time: 5 minutes
Cook Time: 25 minutes

CHEESEBURGER MACARONI

1 cup mostaccioli or elbow macaroni, uncooked
1 pound ground beef
1 medium onion, chopped
1 can (14½ ounces) DEL MONTE® Diced Tomatoes with Basil, Garlic & Oregano
¼ cup DEL MONTE® Tomato Ketchup
1 cup (4 ounces) shredded Cheddar cheese

1. Cook pasta according to package directions; drain.

2. Brown meat with onion in large skillet; drain. Season with salt and pepper, if desired. Stir in tomatoes, ketchup and pasta; heat through.

3. Top with cheese. Garnish, if desired. *Makes 4 servings*

Prep Time: 8 minutes
Cook Time: 15 minutes

MAGIC TIP

To make chopping an onion a less tearful procedure, place the onion in the freezer for 15-20 minutes just before you begin. Also, do the chopping under a stove's exhaust fan, and try wearing some safety goggles purchased from a hardware store.

PASTA BEEF & ZUCCHINI DINNER

1 pound extra lean ground beef
1 medium onion, chopped
1 clove garlic, crushed
½ teaspoon salt
2 (14-ounce) cans ready-to-serve beef broth
1 teaspoon Italian seasoning
¼ teaspoon crushed red pepper
2 cups uncooked mini lasagna or rotini pasta
2 cups sliced zucchini (cut ⅜ inch thick)
1 tablespoon cornstarch
¼ cup water
3 plum tomatoes, each cut into 4 wedges
2 tablespoons grated Parmesan cheese

In large nonstick skillet, cook ground beef with onion, garlic and salt over medium heat 8 to 10 minutes or until beef is browned, stirring occasionally to break up beef into 1-inch crumbles. Remove beef mixture with slotted spoon; set aside. Pour off drippings.

Add broth, Italian seasoning and red pepper to same skillet. Bring to a boil; add pasta. Reduce heat to medium; simmer, uncovered, for 6 minutes, stirring occasionally. Add zucchini; continue cooking an additional 6 to 8 minutes or until pasta is tender, yet firm. Push pasta and zucchini to side of skillet. Mix cornstarch with water and add to broth in skillet; bring to a boil. Return beef mixture to skillet. Add tomatoes; heat through, stirring occasionally. Spoon into serving dish; sprinkle with Parmesan cheese.

Makes 5 servings

*Favorite recipe from **North Dakota Wheat Commission***

CAMPBELL'S® SPICY SALSA MAC & BEEF

1 pound ground beef
1 can (10½ ounces) CAMPBELL'S® Condensed Beef Broth
1⅓ cups water
2 cups *uncooked* medium shell or elbow macaroni
1 can (10¾ ounces) CAMPBELL'S® Condensed Cheddar Cheese Soup
1 cup PACE® Thick & Chunky Salsa

1. In medium skillet over medium-high heat, cook beef until browned, stirring to separate meat. Pour off fat.

2. Add broth and water. Heat to a boil. Stir in macaroni. Reduce heat to medium. Cook 10 minutes or until macaroni is done, stirring often.

3. Stir in soup and salsa and heat through.

Makes 4 servings

Tip: Pair this dynamic kid-pleasing dish with a glass of V8® SPLASH. The light taste of tropical fruit juices makes a great go-with and delivers 100% of Vitamins A and C.

Prep Time: 5 minutes
Cook Time: 25 minutes

CURRY BEEF

12 ounces wide egg noodles *or* 1⅓ cups
   long-grain white rice
1 tablespoon olive oil
1 medium onion, thinly sliced
1 tablespoon curry powder
1 teaspoon ground cumin
2 cloves garlic, minced
1 pound lean ground beef
1 cup (8 ounces) sour cream
½ cup 2% milk
½ cup raisins, divided
1 teaspoon sugar
¼ cup chopped walnuts, almonds or
   pecans

1. Cook noodles or rice according to package directions. Meanwhile, heat oil in large skillet over medium-high heat until hot. Add onion; cook and stir 3 to 4 minutes. Add curry powder, cumin and garlic; cook 2 to 3 minutes longer or until onion is tender. Add meat; cook 6 to 8 minutes or until meat is no longer pink, breaking meat apart with wooden spoon.

2. Stir in sour cream, milk, ¼ cup raisins and sugar. Reduce heat to medium, stirring constantly, until heated through. Spoon over drained noodles or rice. Sprinkle with remaining ¼ cup raisins and nuts.

Makes 4 servings

Serving Suggestion: Serve with sliced cucumber sprinkled with sugar and vinegar or plain yogurt topped with brown sugar, chopped bananas and green onions.

Prep and Cook Time: 30 minutes

TEX-MEX BEEF & BLACK BEAN SKILLET

1 pound lean ground beef or ground
   turkey
1 medium onion, chopped
2 cloves garlic, minced
1 tablespoon Mexican seasoning*
1 (6.8-ounce) package RICE-A-RONI®
   Spanish Rice
2 tablespoons margarine or butter
1 (16-ounce) jar salsa *or* 1 (14½-ounce)
   can diced tomatoes and green chiles,
   undrained
1 (16-ounce) can black beans, rinsed and
   drained
1 cup shredded Monterey Jack cheese or
   jalapeño pepper

**1 teaspoon chili powder, 1 teaspoon ground cumin,
1 teaspoon garlic salt and ¼ teaspoon cayenne pepper may
be substituted.*

1. In large skillet over medium-high heat, cook ground beef, onion and garlic until meat is no longer pink, stirring frequently. Drain; transfer to bowl. Toss with Mexican seasoning; set aside.

2. In same skillet over medium heat, sauté rice-vermicelli mix with margarine until vermicelli is golden brown.

3. Slowly stir in 2 cups water, salsa and Special Seasonings; bring to a boil. Cover; reduce heat to low. Simmer 10 minutes.

4. Stir in beef mixture and beans. Cover; simmer 8 to 10 minutes or until rice is tender. Top with cheese.

Makes 6 servings

Prep Time: 10 minutes
Cook Time: 25 minutes

Curry Beef

TACO POT PIE

1 pound ground beef
1 package (1.25 ounces) taco seasoning
 mix
¼ cup water
1 can (8 ounces) kidney beans, rinsed and
 drained
1 cup chopped tomato
¾ cup frozen corn, thawed
¾ cup frozen peas, thawed
1½ cups (6 ounces) shredded Cheddar
 cheese
1 package (11.5 ounces) refrigerated corn
 bread sticks

1. Preheat oven to 400°F. Brown beef in
medium ovenproof skillet over medium-high
heat, stirring to separate; drain drippings. Add
seasoning mix and water to skillet. Cook over
medium-low heat 3 minutes or until most of
liquid is absorbed, stirring occasionally.

2. Stir in beans, tomato, corn and peas. Cook
3 minutes or until mixture is hot. Remove from
heat; stir in cheese.

3. Unwrap corn bread dough; separate into
16 strips. Twist strips, cutting to fit skillet.
Arrange attractively over meat mixture. Press
ends of dough lightly to edges of skillet to
secure. Bake 15 minutes or until corn bread is
golden brown and meat mixture is bubbly.

Makes 4 to 6 servings

Prep and Cook Time: 30 minutes

CAMPBELL'S® BEEFY MACARONI SKILLET

1 pound ground beef
1 medium onion, chopped (about ½ cup)
1 can (10¾ ounces) CAMPBELL'S®
 Condensed Tomato Soup
¼ cup water
1 tablespoon Worcestershire sauce
½ cup shredded Cheddar cheese (2 ounces)
2 cups cooked corkscrew macaroni (about
 1½ cups uncooked)

1. In medium skillet over medium-high heat,
cook beef and onion until beef is browned,
stirring to separate meat. Pour off fat.

2. Add soup, water, Worcestershire, cheese and
macaroni. Reduce heat to low and heat
through. *Makes 4 servings*

Variation: Substitute 2 cups cooked elbow
macaroni (about 1 cup uncooked) for
corkscrew macaroni.

Tip: This one-skillet family-pleaser works
perfectly as a busy weekday or casual weekend
meal.

Prep Time: 10 minutes
Cook Time: 15 minutes

MAGIC TIP ....

*For the best tomatoes, buy
those that are firm and
uniformly shaped, with a
deep color and pleasant
fragrance. Avoid those that
feel heavy for their size, have
any blemishes or seem too soft
when gently palm-squeezed.*

....

Taco Pot Pie

QUICK GREEK PITAS

1 pound ground beef
1 package (10 ounces) frozen chopped
    spinach, thawed and well drained
4 green onions, chopped
1 can (2¼ ounces) sliced black olives,
    drained
1 teaspoon dried oregano, divided
¼ teaspoon pepper
1 large tomato, diced
1 cup plain nonfat yogurt
½ cup mayonnaise
6 (6-inch) pita breads, warmed
    Lettuce leaves
1 cup (4 ounces) crumbled feta cheese

Cook and stir ground beef in large skillet over
medium-high heat until crumbly and no longer
pink. Drain off drippings. Add spinach, green
onions, olives, ½ teaspoon oregano and pepper;
cook and stir 2 minutes. Stir in tomato.

Combine yogurt, mayonnaise and remaining
½ teaspoon oregano in small bowl. Split open
pita breads; line each with lettuce leaf. Stir
cheese into beef mixture and divide among pita
pockets. Serve with yogurt sauce.

Makes 6 servings

SZECHWAN BEEF

1 pound ground beef
1 tablespoon vegetable oil
1 cup sliced carrots
1 cup frozen peas
⅓ cup water
3 tablespoons soy sauce
2 tablespoons cornstarch
¼ teaspoon ground ginger
1 jar (7 ounces) baby corn
1 medium onion, thinly sliced
    Sliced mushrooms and olives as desired
¼ cup shredded Cheddar cheese
1⅓ cups uncooked instant rice

1. In wok or large skillet, brown ground beef;
remove from wok and set aside. Drain fat.

2. Add oil to wok or skillet and return to
medium heat. Add carrots and peas and stir-fry
about 3 minutes.

3. In small cup, combine water and soy sauce
with cornstarch and ginger. Add to vegetables
in wok.

4. Return ground beef to wok along with baby
corn, onion, mushrooms, olives and cheese.
Cook over medium heat until all ingredients
are heated through.

5. Prepare instant rice according to package
directions. Serve beef and vegetables over rice.

Makes 4 to 5 servings

Favorite recipe from **North Dakota Beef Commission**

CAMPBELL'S® SOUTHWEST SKILLET

¾ pound ground beef
1 tablespoon chili powder
1 can (10¾ ounces) CAMPBELL'S®
    Condensed Beefy Mushroom Soup
¼ cup water
1 can (about 15 ounces) kidney beans,
    rinsed and drained
1 can (14½ ounces) whole peeled
    tomatoes, cut up
¾ cup uncooked Minute® Original Rice
½ cup shredded Cheddar cheese (2 ounces)
    Crumbled tortilla chips

1. In medium skillet over medium-high heat, cook beef and chili powder until browned, stirring to separate meat. Pour off fat.

2. Add soup, water, beans and tomatoes. Heat to a boil. Reduce heat to low. Cover and cook 10 minutes.

3. Stir in rice. Remove from heat. Cover and let stand 5 minutes. Top with cheese and chips.

Makes 4 servings

Prep/Cook Time: 20 minutes
Stand Time: 5 minutes

WESTERN WAGON WHEELS

1 pound lean ground beef or ground
    turkey
2 cups wagon wheel pasta, uncooked
1 can (14½ ounces) stewed tomatoes
1½ cups water
1 box (10 ounces) BIRDS EYE® frozen
    Sweet Corn
½ cup barbecue sauce
    Salt and pepper to taste

• In large skillet, cook beef over medium heat 5 minutes or until well browned.

• Stir in pasta, tomatoes, water, corn and barbecue sauce; bring to a boil.

• Reduce heat to low; cover and simmer 15 to 20 minutes or until pasta is tender, stirring occasionally. Season with salt and pepper.

Makes 4 servings

Serving Suggestion: Serve with corn bread or corn muffins.

Prep Time: 5 minutes
Cook Time: 25 minutes

MAGIC TIP

Store ground meat in the coldest part of the refrigerator (40°F) for up to 2 days. Be sure to always cook ground meat thoroughly until it is browned, to a minimum 155°F.

BROCCOLI AND BEEF PASTA

1 pound lean ground beef
2 cloves garlic, minced
1 can (about 14 ounces) beef broth
1 medium onion, thinly sliced
1 cup uncooked rotini pasta
½ teaspoon dried basil leaves
½ teaspoon dried oregano leaves
½ teaspoon dried thyme leaves
1 can (15 ounces) Italian-style tomatoes, undrained
2 cups broccoli florets *or* 1 package (10 ounces) frozen broccoli, thawed
3 ounces shredded Cheddar cheese or grated Parmesan cheese

1. Combine meat and garlic in large nonstick skillet; cook over high heat until meat is no longer pink, breaking meat apart with wooden spoon. Pour off drippings. Place meat in large bowl; set aside.

2. Add broth, onion, pasta, basil, oregano and thyme to skillet. Bring to a boil. Reduce heat to medium-high and boil 10 minutes (if using frozen broccoli, boil 15 minutes); add tomatoes with juice. Increase heat to high and bring to a boil; stir in broccoli. Cook, uncovered, 6 to 8 minutes, stirring occasionally, until broccoli is crisp-tender and pasta is tender. Return meat to skillet and stir 3 to 4 minutes or until heated through.

3. With slotted spoon, transfer to serving platter. Sprinkle with cheese. Cover with lid or tent with foil several minutes, until cheese melts. Meanwhile, bring liquid left in skillet to a boil over high heat. Boil until thick and reduced to 3 to 4 tablespoons. Spoon over pasta.
Makes 4 servings

Serving Suggestion: Serve with garlic bread.

Prep and Cook Time: 30 minutes

QUICK BEEF STROGANOFF

1 pound ground beef
1 package LIPTON® Noodles & Sauce—Butter
2¼ cups water
1 jar (4½ ounces) sliced mushrooms, drained
2 tablespoons finely chopped pimiento
⅛ teaspoon garlic powder
½ cup sour cream

In 10-inch skillet, brown ground beef; drain. Stir in remaining ingredients except sour cream. Bring to a boil, then simmer, stirring frequently, 7 minutes or until noodles are tender. Stir in sour cream; heat through but do not boil. *Makes about 2 servings*

Microwave Directions: In 2-quart microwavable casserole, cook ground beef at HIGH (Full Power) 4 to 6 minutes. Add noodles & sauce, butter, water, mushrooms, pimiento and garlic powder. Heat at HIGH 10 minutes or until noodles are tender, stirring occasionally. Stir in sour cream.

Broccoli and Beef Pasta

Presto Soups, Stews & Chili

★★★

Albóndigas Soup

1 pound ground beef
¼ cup long-grain rice
1 egg
1 tablespoon chopped fresh cilantro
1 teaspoon LAWRY'S® Seasoned Salt
¼ cup ice water
2 cans (14½ ounces each) chicken broth
1 can (14½ ounces) whole peeled tomatoes, undrained and cut up
1 stalk celery, diced
1 large carrot, diced
1 medium potato, diced
¼ cup chopped onion
¼ teaspoon LAWRY'S® Garlic Powder with Parsley

In medium bowl, combine ground beef, rice, egg, cilantro, Seasoned Salt and ice water; mix well and form into small meatballs. In large saucepan, combine broth, vegetables and Garlic Powder with Parsley. Bring to a boil over medium-high heat; add meatballs. Reduce heat to low; cover and cook 30 to 40 minutes, stirring occasionally. *Makes 6 to 8 servings*

Serving Suggestion: Serve with lemon wedges and warm tortillas.

MAGIC TIP

For a lower-salt version, use homemade or low-sodium chicken broth.

HEARTY CHILI MAC

1 pound lean ground beef
1 can (14½ ounces) diced tomatoes,
    drained
1 cup chopped onion
1 clove garlic, minced
½ teaspoon salt
½ teaspoon ground cumin
½ teaspoon dried oregano leaves
¼ teaspoon black pepper
¼ teaspoon red pepper flakes
1 tablespoon chili powder
2 cups cooked macaroni

Crumble ground beef into slow cooker. Add remaining ingredients, except macaroni, to slow cooker. Cover and cook on LOW 4 hours. Stir in cooked macaroni. Cover and cook on LOW 1 hour.   *Makes 4 servings*

MAGIC TIP

To save time later in the week, double the pasta you make now. Simply drain the extra pasta, place it in ice water to stop further cooking, then drain it again. Toss with about a teaspoon of oil, cover and refrigerate for up to 4 days.

MEXICAN VEGETABLE BEEF SOUP

1 pound ground beef
½ cup chopped onion
1 package (1.0 ounce) LAWRY'S® Taco
    Spices & Seasonings
1 can (28 ounces) whole tomatoes, cut up
1 package (16 ounces) frozen mixed
    vegetables, thawed
1 can (15¼ ounces) kidney beans,
    undrained
1 can (14½ ounces) beef broth
    Corn chips
    Shredded cheddar cheese

In Dutch oven, brown ground beef and onion, stirring until beef is crumbly and onion is tender; drain fat. Add Taco Spices & Seasonings, tomatoes, vegetables, beans and broth. Bring to a boil over medium-high heat; reduce heat to low and cook, uncovered, 5 minutes, stirring occasionally.   *Makes 6 servings*

Serving Suggestion: Top each serving with corn chips and shredded cheddar cheese.

Hint: For extra flavor, add chopped cilantro to beef mixture.

Hearty Chili Mac

TEXAS BEEF STEW

1 pound lean ground beef
1 small onion, chopped
1 can (28 ounces) crushed tomatoes with roasted garlic
1½ cups BIRDS EYE® frozen Farm Fresh Mixtures Broccoli, Cauliflower & Carrots
1 can (14½ ounces) whole new potatoes, halved
1 cup BIRDS EYE® frozen Sweet Corn
1 can (4½ ounces) chopped green chilies, drained
½ cup water

• In large saucepan, cook beef and onion over medium-high heat until beef is well browned, stirring occasionally.

• Stir in tomatoes, vegetables, potatoes with liquid, corn, chilies and water; bring to boil.

• Reduce heat to medium-low; cover and simmer 5 minutes or until heated through.

Makes 4 servings

Serving Suggestion: Serve over rice and with warm crusty bread.

Prep Time: 5 minutes
Cook Time: 15 minutes

QUICK & EASY CHILI

1 pound ground beef
1 cup (1 small) chopped onion
2 cloves garlic, finely chopped
3½ cups (two 15-ounce cans) kidney, pinto or black beans, drained
2½ cups (24-ounce jar) ORTEGA® Thick & Chunky Salsa, hot, medium or mild
½ cup (4-ounce can) ORTEGA® Diced Green Chiles
2 teaspoons chili powder
½ teaspoon dried oregano, crushed
½ teaspoon ground cumin
Topping suggestions: ORTEGA® Thick and Chunky Salsa, shredded Cheddar cheese or Monterey Jack cheese, chopped tomatoes, sliced ripe olives, sliced green onions and sour cream

COOK beef, onion and garlic in large skillet over medium-high heat for 4 to 5 minutes or until beef is no longer pink; drain.

STIR in beans, salsa, chiles, chili powder, oregano and cumin. Bring to a boil. Reduce heat to low; cook, covered, for 20 to 25 minutes.

TOP as desired before serving.

Makes 6 servings

MAGIC TIP ....

The smell of onions and garlic can penetrate into your cutting boards. Keep a separate cutting board exclusively for these vegetables.

Texas Beef Stew

DURANGO CHILI

3 tablespoons vegetable oil, divided
1 pound lean ground beef
1 pound lean boneless beef, cut into
    ½-inch cubes
2 medium onions, chopped
1 green bell pepper, seeded and chopped
4 cloves garlic, minced
¼ cup tomato paste
3 to 5 fresh or canned jalapeño peppers,*
    stemmed, seeded and minced
2 bay leaves
5 tablespoons chili powder
1 teaspoon salt
1 teaspoon ground cumin
½ teaspoon black pepper
2 cans (14½ ounces each) tomatoes,
    undrained
1 bottle (12 ounces) beer
1 can (10¾ ounces) condensed beef broth
    plus 1 can water
2 cans (4 ounces each) diced green chilies,
    undrained
3 cups cooked pinto beans *or* 2 cans
    (15 ounces each) pinto or kidney
    beans, drained

CONDIMENTS
1 cup (4 ounces) shredded Cheddar cheese
½ cup sour cream
4 green onions with tops, thinly sliced
1 can (2¼ ounces) sliced pitted ripe olives,
    drained

Jalapeño peppers can sting and irritate the skin; wear rubber gloves when handling peppers and do not touch eyes. Wash hands after handling peppers.

Heat 1 tablespoon of the oil in 5-quart kettle over medium-high heat. Crumble in ground beef; add cubed beef. Cook, stirring occasionally, until meat is lightly browned. Transfer meat and pan drippings to a medium bowl. Heat the remaining 2 tablespoons oil in kettle over medium heat. Add onions, bell pepper and garlic. Cook until vegetables are tender. Stir in tomato paste, jalapeño peppers, bay leaves, chili powder, salt, cumin and black pepper. Coarsely chop tomatoes; add to kettle.

Add meat, beer, beef broth, water and green chilies. Bring to a boil. Reduce heat and simmer, partially covered, 2 hours or until meat is very tender and chili has thickened slightly. Stir in beans. Continue simmering, uncovered, 20 minutes. If you prefer thicker chili, continue simmering, uncovered, until chili is of desired consistency. Discard bay leaves. Spoon into individual bowls. Serve with condiments.

Makes 6 servings

HEARTY BEEF STEW

1 pound ground beef
1 tablespoon minced garlic
1 jar (14 ounces) marinara sauce
1 can (10½ ounces) condensed beef broth
1 package (16 ounces) Italian-style frozen
    vegetables
2 cups southern-style hash brown potatoes
2 tablespoons *French's*® Worcestershire
    Sauce
2 cups *French's*® *Taste Toppers*™ French
    Fried Onions

1. Brown beef with garlic in large saucepan until no longer pink; drain. Add marinara sauce, broth, vegetables, potatoes and Worcestershire. Bring to boiling; cover. Reduce heat to medium-low. Cook 10 minutes or until vegetables are crisp-tender.

2. Spoon soup into bowls. Sprinkle with *Taste Toppers*. Serve with garlic bread, if desired.

Makes 6 servings

Prep Time: 5 minutes
Cook Time: 15 minutes

HANOI BEEF AND RICE SOUP

1½ pounds ground chuck
2 tablespoons cold water
2 tablespoons soy sauce
2 teaspoons sugar
2 teaspoons cornstarch
2 teaspoons lime juice
½ teaspoon black pepper
2 cloves garlic, minced
2 teaspoons fennel seeds
1 teaspoon anise seeds
1 cinnamon stick (3 inches long)
2 bay leaves
6 whole cloves
1 tablespoon vegetable oil
1 cup uncooked long-grain white rice
1 medium yellow onion, sliced and separated into rings
1 tablespoon minced fresh ginger
4 cans (about 14 ounces each) beef broth
2 cups water
½ pound fresh snow peas, trimmed
1 fresh red Thai chili or red jalapeño pepper,* cut into slivers, for garnish

Thai chilies and jalapeño peppers can sting and irritate the skin; wear rubber gloves when handling chilies and do not touch eyes. Wash hands after handling peppers.

1. Combine beef, 2 tablespoons water, soy sauce, sugar, cornstarch, lime juice, black pepper and garlic in large bowl; mix well. Place meat mixture on cutting board; pat evenly into 1-inch-thick square. Cut meat into 36 squares; shape each square into a ball.

2. Bring 4 inches water to a boil in wok over high heat. Add meatballs and return water to a boil. Cook meatballs 3 to 4 minutes or until firm, stirring occasionally. Using a slotted spoon, transfer meatballs to bowl. Discard water.

3. Place fennel seeds, anise seeds, cinnamon, bay leaves and cloves on 12-inch double-thick square of dampened cheesecloth. Tie with string to create spice bag; set aside.

4. Heat wok over medium heat 1 minute or until hot. Drizzle oil into wok and heat 30 seconds. Add rice; cook and stir 3 to 4 minutes or until lightly browned. Add onion and ginger. Stir-fry 1 minute. Add beef broth, 2 cups water and spice bag. Cover and bring to a boil. Reduce heat to low; simmer 25 minutes.

5. Remove spice bag and discard. Add meatballs and snow peas to soup. Cook and stir until heated through. Ladle soup into tureen or individual serving bowls. Garnish, if desired.
Makes 6 main-dish servings

SPICY QUICK AND EASY CHILI

1 pound ground beef
1 large clove garlic, minced
1 can (15¼ ounces) DEL MONTE® Whole Kernel Golden Sweet Corn, drained
1 can (16 ounces) kidney beans, drained
1½ cups salsa, mild, medium or hot
1 can (4 ounces) diced green chiles, undrained

1. Brown meat with garlic in large saucepan; drain.

2. Add remaining ingredients. Simmer, uncovered, 10 minutes, stirring occasionally. Sprinkle with chopped green onions, if desired.
Makes 4 servings

Prep and Cook Time: 15 minutes

CLASSIC MEATBALL SOUP

2 pounds beef bones
3 ribs celery
2 carrots
1 medium onion, cut in half
1 bay leaf
6 cups cold water
1 egg
4 tablespoons chopped fresh parsley, divided
1 teaspoon salt, divided
½ teaspoon dried marjoram leaves, crushed
¼ teaspoon black pepper, divided
½ cup soft fresh bread crumbs
¼ cup grated Parmesan cheese
1 pound ground beef
1 can (14½ ounces) whole peeled tomatoes, undrained
½ cup uncooked rotini or small macaroni

1. To make stock, rinse beef bones and combine with celery, carrots, onion and bay leaf in 6-quart stockpot. Add water. Bring to a boil; reduce heat to low. Cover partially and simmer 1 hour, skimming foam occasionally.

2. Preheat oven to 400°F. Spray 13×9-inch baking pan with nonstick cooking spray. Combine egg, 3 tablespoons parsley, ½ teaspoon salt, marjoram and ⅛ teaspoon pepper in medium bowl; whisk lightly. Stir in bread crumbs and cheese. Add beef; mix well. Place meat mixture on cutting board; pat evenly into 1-inch-thick square. With sharp knife, cut meat into 1-inch squares; shape each square into a ball. Place meatballs in prepared pan; bake 20 to 25 minutes until brown on all sides and cooked through, turning occasionally. Drain on paper towels.

3. Strain stock through sieve into medium bowl. Slice celery and carrots; reserve. Discard bones, onion and bay leaf. To degrease stock, let stand 5 minutes to allow fat to rise. Holding paper towel, quickly pull across surface only, allowing towel to absorb fat. Discard. Repeat with clean paper towels as many times as needed to remove all fat.

4. Return stock to stockpot. Drain tomatoes, reserving juice. Chop tomatoes; add to stock with juice. Bring to a boil; boil 5 minutes. Stir in rotini, remaining ½ teaspoon salt and ⅛ teaspoon pepper. Cook 6 minutes, stirring occasionally. Add reserved vegetables and meatballs. Reduce heat to medium; cook 10 minutes until hot. Stir in remaining 1 tablespoon parsley. Season to taste.

Makes 4 to 6 servings

CHILI BEEF MAC

1 pound lean ground beef or ground turkey
4 teaspoons Mexican seasoning*
⅔ cup milk
1 (4.8-ounce) package PASTA RONI® Four Cheese Flavor with Corkscrew Pasta
1 medium green, red or yellow bell pepper, diced
½ cup salsa
¼ cup chopped cilantro or sliced green onions

2 teaspoons chili powder, 1 teaspoon ground cumin and 1 teaspoon garlic salt may be substituted.

1. In large skillet over medium-high heat, cook ground beef and Mexican seasoning for 5 minutes, stirring occasionally.

2. Add 1¼ cups water, milk, pasta, bell pepper, salsa and Special Seasonings. Bring to a boil. Reduce heat to low. Cover; simmer 8 to 9 minutes or until pasta is tender. Stir in cilantro. Let stand 5 minutes before serving.

Makes 4 servings

Prep Time: 5 minutes
Cook Time: 20 minutes

Classic Meatball Soup

RAPID RAGÚ® CHILI

1½ pounds lean ground beef
1 medium onion, chopped
2 tablespoons chili powder
1 can (19 ounces) red kidney beans, rinsed
    and drained
1 jar (26 to 28 ounces) RAGÚ® Old World
    Style® Pasta Sauce
1 cup shredded Cheddar cheese (about
    4 ounces)

1. In 12-inch skillet, brown ground beef with
onion and chili powder over medium-high heat,
stirring occasionally. Stir in beans and Ragú
Pasta Sauce.

2. Bring to a boil over high heat. Reduce heat
to low and simmer covered, stirring
occasionally, 20 minutes. Top with cheese.
Serve, if desired, over hot cooked rice.

Makes 6 servings

Prep Time: 10 minutes
Cook Time: 25 minutes

MAGIC TIP

*Form meatballs easily and
without a mess by spooning
the beef mixture between
sheets of plastic wrap and
rolling into the desired shape.*

MINESTRONE SOUP WITH MINI MEATBALLS

1 pound ground beef or ground turkey
1 teaspoon dried Italian seasoning
½ teaspoon garlic powder, divided
2 tablespoons vegetable oil, divided
5 cups assorted fresh vegetables*
1 envelope LIPTON® RECIPE SECRETS®
    Onion Soup Mix
4 cups water
1 can (28 ounces) Italian plum tomatoes,
    undrained
1 teaspoon sugar

*Use any of the following to equal 5 cups: green beans, cut
into 1-inch pieces; diced zucchini; diced carrot; or diced
celery.*

In medium bowl, combine ground beef, Italian
seasoning and ¼ teaspoon garlic powder. Shape
into 1-inch meatballs.

In 6-quart Dutch oven or heavy saucepan, heat
1 tablespoon oil over medium-high heat and
brown meatballs. Remove meatballs. Heat
remaining 1 tablespoon oil in same Dutch oven
and cook vegetables, stirring frequently,
5 minutes or until crisp-tender. Stir in soup mix
blended with water, remaining ¼ teaspoon
garlic powder, tomatoes and sugar. Bring to a
boil over high heat, breaking up tomatoes with
wooden spoon. Reduce heat to low and simmer
covered 25 minutes. Return meatballs to skillet.
Continue simmering covered 5 minutes or until
meatballs are heated through. Serve with
grated Parmesan cheese and garlic bread, if
desired. *Makes 6 servings*

Rapid Ragú® Chili

FARMER'S STEW ARGENTINA

3 cups water
1 pound lean ground beef
2 tablespoons vegetable oil
1 medium onion, chopped
1 green bell pepper, cut into ½-inch pieces
1 red bell pepper, cut into ½-inch pieces
1 small sweet potato, peeled and cut into ½-inch pieces
1 large clove garlic, minced
1 tablespoon chopped fresh parsley
1 teaspoon salt
½ teaspoon granulated sugar
⅛ teaspoon ground cumin
3 cups beef broth, heated
½ pound zucchini, cut into ½-inch pieces
1 cup whole kernel corn
2 tablespoons raisins
1 teaspoon TABASCO® brand Pepper Sauce
1 small pear, firm but ripe, cut into 1-inch pieces
6 cups cooked white rice

Bring water to a boil in large saucepan. Remove saucepan from heat. Add ground beef, stirring to break meat into little pieces. Let stand 5 minutes, stirring once or twice, until most of the pink disappears from meat. Drain meat well, discarding water.

Heat oil in large deep skillet or Dutch oven over medium-high heat. Add onion and cook 4 to 5 minutes, stirring constantly, until limp and slightly brown. Add beef. Continue cooking, stirring constantly, until all liquid has evaporated from pan and meat is lightly browned, about 10 minutes.

Reduce heat to medium. Add bell peppers, sweet potato and garlic. Continue cooking and stirring 5 minutes, or until peppers and potatoes are slightly tender. Add parsley, salt, sugar and cumin. Stir and cook 1 minute to blend flavors. Pour beef broth into skillet. Add zucchini, corn, raisins and TABASCO® Sauce. Simmer gently 10 minutes, being careful not to

boil. Add pear and simmer 10 additional minutes, or until all fruits and vegetables are tender. Ladle over rice in individual serving bowls. *Makes 6 servings*

TEXAS-STYLE CHILI

1½ pounds ground beef or cubed round steak
1 green bell pepper, diced
1 onion, diced
1 can (2.25 ounces) diced green chiles, drained
1 package (1.48 ounces) LAWRY'S® Spices & Seasonings for Chili
1½ tablespoons cornmeal
1 tablespoon chili powder
1 teaspoon sugar
¼ to ½ teaspoon cayenne pepper
1 can (14½ ounces) diced tomatoes, undrained
¾ cup water
Sour cream (optional)
Shredded cheddar cheese (optional)

In Dutch oven or large saucepan, cook beef until browned and crumbly; drain beef, reserving fat; set beef aside. Cook bell pepper and onion in Dutch oven with reserved fat over medium-high heat 5 minutes or until vegetables are crisp-tender. Return beef to Dutch oven. Add chiles, Spices & Seasonings for Chili, cornmeal, chili powder, sugar and cayenne pepper; mix well. Stir in tomatoes and water. Bring to a boil over medium-high heat; reduce heat to low, cover and simmer 30 minutes, stirring occasionally.

Makes 4½ cups

Serving Suggestion: Serve topped with sour cream or cheddar cheese, if desired.

Hint: This recipe is perfect for leftover meat. Use 3½ cups shredded beef. If using shredded beef or cubed round steak, brown in 1 tablespoon vegetable oil.

WILD RICE SOUP

½ cup uncooked wild rice
1 pound lean ground beef
1 can (14½ ounces) chicken broth
1 can (10¾ ounces) condensed cream of
    mushroom soup
2 cups milk
1 cup (4 ounces) shredded Cheddar cheese
⅓ cup shredded carrot
1 package (.4 ounce) HIDDEN VALLEY®
    Buttermilk Recipe Original Ranch®
    salad dressing mix
Chopped green onions with tops

Cook rice according to package directions to
make about 1½ cups cooked rice. In Dutch oven
or large saucepan, brown beef; drain off excess
fat. Stir in rice, chicken broth, cream of
mushroom soup, milk, cheese, carrot and dry
salad dressing mix. Heat to a simmer over low
heat, stirring occasionally, about 15 minutes.
Serve in warmed soup bowls; top with green
onions. Garnish with additional green onions, if
desired.   *Makes 6 to 8 servings*

MAGIC TIP

*Avoid ground beef with a bad
odor, discolored patches
(usually gray or brown) or
browned or dry-looking
edges. When unsure if beef is
fresh, apply the cook's saying:
"If in doubt, throw it out."*

MEATY CHILI

1 pound coarsely ground beef
¼ pound ground Italian sausage
1 large onion, chopped
2 medium ribs celery, diced
2 fresh jalapeño peppers,* chopped
2 cloves garlic, minced
1 can (28 ounces) whole peeled tomatoes,
    undrained, cut up
1 can (15 ounces) pinto beans, drained
1 can (12 ounces) tomato juice
1 cup water
¼ cup ketchup
1 teaspoon sugar
1 teaspoon chili powder
½ teaspoon salt
½ teaspoon ground cumin
½ teaspoon dried thyme leaves
⅛ teaspoon black pepper

*Jalapeño peppers can sting and irritate the skin; wear
rubber gloves when handling peppers and do not touch eyes.
Wash hands after handling.*

Cook beef, sausage, onion, celery, jalapeños
and garlic in 5-quart Dutch oven over medium-
high heat until meat is browned and onion is
tender, stirring frequently.

Stir in tomatoes with liquid, beans, tomato
juice, water, ketchup, sugar, chili powder, salt,
cumin, thyme and black pepper. Bring to a boil
over high heat. Reduce heat to medium-low;
simmer, uncovered, 30 minutes, stirring
occasionally.

Ladle into bowls. Garnish, if desired.
                                  Makes 6 servings

ALL-IN-ONE BURGER STEW

1 pound lean ground beef
2 cups frozen Italian vegetables
1 can (14½ ounces) chopped tomatoes
    with basil and garlic
1 can (about 14 ounces) beef broth
2½ cups uncooked medium egg noodles
    Salt

1. Cook meat in Dutch oven or large skillet over medium-high heat until no longer pink, breaking meat apart with wooden spoon. Drain drippings.

2. Add vegetables, tomatoes and broth; bring to a boil over high heat.

3. Add noodles; reduce heat to medium. Cover and cook 12 to 15 minutes or until noodles have absorbed liquid and vegetables are tender. Add salt and pepper to taste.   *Makes 6 servings*

For a special touch, sprinkle with chopped parsley before serving.

Tip: To complete this meal, serve with breadsticks or a loaf of Italian bread and a mixed green and tomato salad.

Prep and Cook Time: 25 minutes

RIVERBOAT CHILI

2 pounds lean ground beef
2 large onions, chopped
1 large green pepper, chopped
2 cans (14½ ounces each) FRANK'S® or
    SNOWFLOSS® Original Style Diced
    Tomatoes, undrained
1 can (14½ ounces) FRANK'S® or
    SNOWFLOSS® Stewed Tomatoes,
    undrained
⅓ cup MISSISSIPPI® Barbecue Sauce
2 bay leaves
3 whole cloves
2 teaspoons chili powder
½ teaspoon cayenne pepper
½ teaspoon paprika
4 cans (15½ ounces each) dark red kidney
    beans

1. Brown ground beef in large stock pot. Drain grease.

2. Add onions, green pepper, diced tomatoes, stewed tomatoes, barbecue sauce, bay leaves, cloves, chili powder, cayenne pepper and paprika. Stir well.

3. Add kidney beans and stir well.

4. Cover and simmer 2 hours, stirring occasionally.   *Makes 4 to 6 servings*

Microwave Directions: Crumble beef into large microwavable casserole dish. Cook uncovered about 6 minutes, stirring at least twice to break up meat. Drain grease. Add onions, green pepper, diced tomatoes, stewed tomatoes, barbecue sauce, bay leaves, cloves, chili powder, cayenne pepper and paprika. Cook 1 minute. Stir well. Add kidney beans and stir well. Cover and cook 15 to 20 minutes, stirring occasionally. Cover and let stand 5 minutes.

Prep Time: 30 minutes
Cook Time: 2 hours

All-in-One Burger Stew

IN A FLASH

★★★

SALISBURY STEAKS WITH MUSHROOM-WINE SAUCE

  1 pound lean ground beef sirloin
¾ teaspoon garlic salt or seasoned salt
¼ teaspoon black pepper
  2 tablespoons butter or margarine
  1 package (8 ounces) sliced button mushrooms or 2 packages (4 ounces each) sliced exotic mushrooms
  2 tablespoons sweet vermouth or ruby port wine
  1 jar (12 ounces) or 1 can (10½ ounces) beef gravy

1. Heat large heavy nonstick skillet over medium-high heat 3 minutes or until hot.* Meanwhile, combine ground sirloin, garlic salt and pepper; mix well. Shape mixture into four ¼-inch-thick oval-shaped patties.

2. Place patties in skillet as they are formed; cook 3 minutes per side or until browned and heated through. Transfer to plate. Pour off drippings.

3. Melt butter in skillet; add mushrooms. Cook and stir 2 minutes. Add vermouth; cook 1 minute. Add gravy; mix well.

4. Return patties to skillet; simmer, uncovered, over medium heat 2 minutes for medium or until desired doneness, turning meat and stirring sauce.

Makes 4 servings

*If pan is not heavy, use medium heat.

Note: For a special touch, sprinkle steaks with chopped parsley or chives.

Prep and Cook Time: 20 minutes

CRUNCHY LAYERED BEEF & BEAN SALAD

1 pound ground beef or turkey
2 cans (15 to 19 ounces *each*) black beans
    or pinto beans, rinsed and drained
1 can (14½ ounces) stewed tomatoes,
    undrained
1½ cups *French's® Taste Toppers™* French
    Fried Onions, divided
1 package (1¼ ounces) taco seasoning mix
1 tablespoon *Frank's® RedHot®* Sauce
6 cups shredded lettuce
1 cup (4 ounces) shredded Cheddar or
    Monterey Jack cheese

1. Cook beef in large nonstick skillet over medium heat until thoroughly browned; drain well. Stir in beans, tomatoes, ⅔ cup *Taste Toppers*, taco seasoning and *RedHot* Sauce. Heat to boiling. Cook over medium heat 5 minutes, stirring occasionally.

2. Spoon beef mixture over lettuce on serving platter. Top with cheese.

3. Microwave remaining *1 cup Taste Toppers* 1 minute on HIGH. Sprinkle over salad.

Makes 6 servings

Ultimate Pretzel Dip: Combine ½ cup *French's®* Honey Mustard **Grill & Glaze** Sauce with *French's® Classic Yellow Mustard®*, Dijon or Deli Mustard. Use for dipping pretzels, chips or cheese cubes.

Prep Time: 10 minutes
Cook Time: 6 minutes

SONOMA BURGERS STUFFED WITH BLUE CHEESE

½ pound ground beef or meat of your
    choice
  Salt and pepper
1 tablespoon Worcestershire sauce
2 ounces blue cheese, divided
8 SONOMA® Marinated Tomatoes,
    chopped
½ medium yellow onion, finely chopped

Season meat lightly with salt and pepper. Mix in Worcestershire sauce; halve the meat mixture and form into two patties. Carve a cavity into the center of each patty, stuff with blue cheese and reseal the patty exterior to keep cheese inside. Set aside.

Heat a non-stick skillet over medium-high heat until hot. Heat marinated tomatoes with some of their oil and the onion until mixture sizzles. Push mixture aside and add the two patties; let meat sear to seal in juices, then reduce heat to medium. Cover pan; cook 2 to 2½ minutes on each side. Add a pinch more of salt and pepper during last minutes of cooking. Serve each burger on toasted bread, if desired. Garnish with tomatoes and onions.

Makes 2 servings

Prep Time: 5 minutes
Cooking Time: 8 minutes

Crunchy Layered Beef & Bean Salad

FAST 'N' EASY CHILI

1½ pounds ground beef
  1 envelope LIPTON® RECIPE SECRETS®
    Onion Soup Mix*
  1 can (15 to 19 ounces) red kidney or black
    beans, drained
1½ cups water
  1 can (8 ounces) tomato sauce
  4 teaspoons chili powder

*Also terrific with LIPTON® RECIPE SECRETS® Beefy
Mushroom, Onion-Mushroom, Beefy Onion or Fiesta Herb
with Red Pepper Soup Mix.*

1. In 12-inch skillet, brown ground beef over
medium-high heat; drain.

2. Stir in remaining ingredients. Bring to a boil
over high heat. Reduce heat to low and simmer
covered, stirring occasionally, 20 minutes.
Serve, if desired, over hot cooked rice.
Makes 6 servings

First Alarm Chili: Add 5 teaspoons chili
powder.

Second Alarm Chili: Add 2 tablespoons chili
powder.

Third Alarm Chili: Add chili powder at your
own risk.

CREAMY BEEF AND VEGETABLE CASSEROLE

1 pound lean ground beef
1 small onion, chopped
1 bag (16 ounces) BIRDS EYE® frozen
    Farm Fresh Mixtures Broccoli, Corn &
    Red Peppers
1 can (10¾ ounces) cream of mushroom
    soup

• In medium skillet, brown beef and onion;
drain excess fat.

• Meanwhile, in large saucepan, cook
vegetables according to package directions;
drain.

• Stir in beef mixture and soup. Cook over
medium heat until heated through.
Makes 4 servings

Serving Suggestion: Serve over rice and
sprinkle with ½ cup shredded Cheddar cheese.

Prep Time: 5 minutes
Cook Time: 10 to 15 minutes

MAGIC TIP

*Keep spices fresh by storing
them in airtight containers
kept in a dark, cool place for
up to 6 months. Chili powder
and other spice blends should
never be kept over a stove or
other warm area, as they will
lose their flavor sooner.*

SLOPPY JOE ROLLERS

1 small onion, finely chopped
¼ cup finely chopped red bell pepper
1½ pounds ground beef
¾ cup chili sauce
2 tablespoons *French's*® Worcestershire
    Sauce
1⅓ cups *French's® Taste Toppers™* French
    Fried Onions
1 cup shredded Cheddar cheese
8 (10-inch) flour tortillas, heated

1. Heat *1 tablespoon oil* in 12-inch nonstick skillet over medium-high heat. Cook onion and red pepper 2 minutes. Stir in meat and cook 5 minutes or until browned; drain. Stir in chili sauce and Worcestershire. Simmer 3 minutes.

2. To serve, arrange meat mixture, ***Taste Toppers*** and cheese down center of tortillas, dividing evenly. Fold bottom third of each tortilla over filling; fold sides towards center. Tightly roll up to secure filling. Cut in half to serve.   *Makes 8 servings*

Prep Time: 5 minutes
Cook Time: 10 minutes

QUICK 'N' EASY TACOS

1 pound ground beef
1 can (14½ ounces) whole peeled
    tomatoes, undrained and coarsely
    chopped
1 medium green bell pepper, finely
    chopped
1 envelope LIPTON® RECIPE SECRETS®
    Onion Soup Mix*
1 tablespoon chili powder
3 drops hot pepper sauce (optional)
8 taco shells
  Taco Toppings

*Also terrific with Lipton® Recipe Secrets® Onion-Mushroom or Beefy Mushroom Soup Mix.

In medium skillet, brown ground beef over medium-high heat; drain. Stir in tomatoes, green pepper, onion soup mix, chili powder and hot pepper sauce, if using. Bring to a boil, then simmer 15 minutes or until slightly thickened. Serve in taco shells with assorted Taco Toppings.   *Makes 4 servings*

Taco Toppings: Use shredded Cheddar or Monterey Jack cheese, shredded lettuce, chopped tomatoes, sliced pitted ripe olives, sour cream or taco sauce.

MINI MEXICAN BURGER BITES

1½ pounds ground beef
½ cup finely chopped red, yellow or green
    bell pepper
2 tablespoons *French's*® Worcestershire
    Sauce
1 teaspoon *Frank's*® *RedHot*® Sauce
1 teaspoon dried oregano leaves
¼ teaspoon salt
12 mini dinner rolls
    Shredded Cheddar cheese

1. Gently combine all ingredients except rolls
and cheese in large bowl. Shape into 12 mini
patties. Broil or grill patties 4 to 6 minutes for
medium doneness (160°F internal
temperature), turning once.

2. Arrange burgers on rolls and top with
Cheddar cheese. Top with shredded lettuce,
if desired.   *Makes 6 servings*

Prep Time: 5 minutes
Cook Time: 8 minutes

TACO TATERS

1 pound ground beef
1 jar (26 to 28 ounces) RAGÚ® Old World
    Style® Pasta Sauce
1 package (1.25 ounces) taco seasoning
    mix
6 large all-purpose potatoes, unpeeled and
    baked

1. In 12-inch skillet, brown ground beef over
medium-high heat; drain. Stir in Ragú Pasta
Sauce and taco seasoning mix and cook
5 minutes.

2. To serve, cut a lengthwise slice from top of
each potato. Evenly spoon beef mixture onto
each potato. Garnish, if desired, with shredded
Cheddar cheese and sour cream.
                Makes 6 servings

Prep Time: 5 minutes
Cook Time: 15 minutes

CAMPBELL'S® EASY SKILLET BEEF & HASH BROWNS

1 pound ground beef
1 can (10¾ ounces) CAMPBELL'S®
    Condensed Cream of Celery Soup *or*
    98% Fat Free Cream of Celery Soup
½ cup water
¼ cup ketchup
1 tablespoon Worcestershire sauce
2 cups frozen diced potatoes
    (hash browns)
3 slices process American cheese
    (about 3 ounces)

1. In medium skillet over medium-high heat,
cook beef until browned, stirring to separate
meat. Pour off fat.

2. Add soup, water, ketchup and Worcestershire.
Heat to a boil. Stir in potatoes. Reduce heat to
medium-low. Cover and cook 10 minutes or
until potatoes are done, stirring occasionally.
Top with cheese.   *Makes 4 servings*

Prep/Cook Time: 20 minutes

Mini Mexican Burger Bites

SWEET AND SOUR BEEF

1 pound lean ground beef
1 small onion, thinly sliced
2 teaspoons minced fresh ginger
1 package (16 ounces) frozen mixed
   vegetables (snap peas, carrots, water
   chestnuts, pineapple, red pepper)
6 to 8 tablespoons bottled sweet and sour
   sauce or sauce from vegetable mix
   Cooked rice

1. Place beef, onion and ginger in large skillet;
cook over high heat 6 to 8 minutes or until no
longer pink, breaking apart with wooden spoon.
Drain drippings.

2. Stir in frozen vegetables and sauce. Cook,
covered, 6 to 8 minutes, stirring every
2 minutes or until vegetables are heated
through. Serve over rice.   *Makes 4 servings*

Serving Suggestion: Serve with sliced Asian
apple-pears.

Prep and Cook Time: 15 minutes

MAGIC TIP

*Squeezing small chunks of
peeled fresh ginger root in a
garlic press is a fast and easy
way to get minced ginger.*

GROOVY ANGEL HAIR GOULASH

1 pound lean ground beef
2 tablespoons margarine or butter
1 (4.8-ounce) package PASTA RONI® Angel
   Hair Pasta with Herbs
1 (14½-ounce) can diced tomatoes,
   undrained
1 cup frozen or canned corn, drained

1. In large skillet over medium-high heat,
brown ground beef. Remove from skillet; drain.
Set aside.

2. In same skillet, bring 1½ cups water and
margarine to a boil.

3. Stir in pasta; cook 1 minute or just until
pasta softens slightly. Stir in tomatoes, corn,
beef and Special Seasonings; return to a boil.
Reduce heat to medium. Gently boil, uncovered,
4 to 5 minutes or until pasta is tender, stirring
frequently. Let stand 3 to 5 minutes before
serving.   *Makes 4 servings*

Prep Time: 5 minutes
Cook Time: 15 minutes

Sweet and Sour Beef

BITE SIZE TACOS

1 pound ground beef
1 package (1.25 ounces) taco seasoning
    mix
2 cups *French's® Taste Toppers™* French
    Fried Onions
¼ cup chopped fresh cilantro
32 bite-size round tortilla chips
¾ cup sour cream
1 cup shredded Cheddar cheese

1. Cook beef in nonstick skillet over medium-high heat 5 minutes or until browned; drain. Stir in taco seasoning mix, *¾ cup water, 1 cup Taste Toppers* and cilantro. Simmer 5 minutes or until flavors are blended, stirring often.

2. Preheat oven to 350°F. Arrange tortilla chips on foil-lined baking sheet. Top with beef mixture, sour cream, remaining *Taste Toppers* and cheese.

3. Bake 5 minutes or until cheese is melted and *Taste Toppers* are golden.

Makes 8 appetizer servings

Prep Time: 5 minutes
Cook Time: 15 minutes

CORNY SLOPPY JOES

1 pound lean ground beef or ground
    turkey
1 small onion, chopped
1 can (15½ ounces) sloppy joe sauce
1 box (10 ounces) BIRDS EYE® frozen
    Sweet Corn
6 hamburger buns

• In large skillet, cook beef and onion over high heat until beef is well browned.

• Stir in sloppy joe sauce and corn; reduce heat to low and simmer 5 minutes or until heated through.

• Serve mixture in hamburger buns.

Makes 6 servings

Serving Suggestion: Sprinkle with shredded Cheddar cheese.

Prep Time: 5 minutes
Cook Time: 15 minutes

WESTERN HASH

1 pound ground beef
1 can (28 ounces) tomatoes, undrained
1 cup long-grain rice, uncooked
1 cup chopped green pepper
½ cup chopped onion
½ pound (8 ounces) VELVEETA®
   Pasteurized Prepared Cheese Product,
   sliced

BROWN meat in large skillet on medium-high heat; drain.

ADD tomatoes, rice, green pepper and onion; cover. Reduce heat to medium-low; simmer 25 minutes.

TOP with VELVEETA; continue cooking until VELVEETA is melted.   *Makes 6 servings*

Prep Time: 10 minutes

CAMPBELL'S® QUICK BEEF SKILLET

1 pound ground beef
1 can (10¾ ounces) CAMPBELL'S®
   Condensed Tomato Soup
¼ cup water
1 tablespoon Worcestershire sauce
¼ teaspoon pepper
1 can (about 15 ounces) sliced potatoes,
   drained
1 can (about 8 ounces) sliced carrots,
   drained

1. In medium skillet over medium-high heat, cook beef until browned, stirring to separate meat. Pour off fat.

2. Add soup, water, Worcestershire, pepper, potatoes and carrots. Reduce heat to low and heat through.   *Makes 4 servings*

Prep/Cook Time: 15 minutes

NACHO BACHO

1½ pounds ground beef
1 cup chunky hot salsa
½ cup salad dressing
2 tablespoons Italian seasoning
1 tablespoon chili powder
2 cups (8 ounces) shredded Colby-Jack
   cheese
3 cups nacho-flavored tortilla chips,
   crushed
1 cup sour cream
½ cup sliced black olives

Brown ground beef in skillet over medium heat; drain. In medium bowl, combine salsa, salad dressing, Italian seasoning and chili powder. Add beef. Place in 11×7-inch baking dish. Top with 1 cup cheese. Cover with crushed chips and remaining cheese. Bake at 350°F 20 minutes. Garnish with sour cream and sliced olives.   *Makes 4 servings*

*Favorite recipe from **North Dakota Beef Commission***

MAGIC TIP

To store fresh salsa, cover it tightly and refrigerate for up to 4 days. In addition to adding an exciting, spicy flavor to many Southwestern dishes, it can be used as a tasty topping for scrambled eggs, hash browns or hamburgers.

BEEFY BEAN & WALNUT STIR-FRY

1 teaspoon vegetable oil
3 cloves garlic, minced
1 pound lean ground beef or ground
    turkey
1 bag (16 ounces) BIRDS EYE® frozen Cut
    Green Beans, thawed
1 teaspoon salt
½ cup walnut pieces

• In large skillet, heat oil and garlic over medium heat about 30 seconds.

• Add beef and beans; sprinkle with salt. Mix well.

• Cook 5 minutes or until beef is well browned, stirring occasionally.

• Stir in walnuts; cook 2 minutes more.

Makes 4 servings

Serving Suggestion: Serve over hot cooked egg noodles or rice.

Birds Eye Idea: When you add California walnuts to Birds Eye® vegetables, you not only add texture and a great nutty taste, but nutrition, too.

Prep Time: 5 minutes
Cook Time: 7 to 10 minutes

CAMPBELL'S® BEEF & CHEDDAR SOFT TACOS

1 pound ground beef
1 can (10¾ ounces) CAMPBELL'S®
    Condensed Cheddar Cheese Soup
½ cup PACE® Thick & Chunky Salsa *or*
    Picante Sauce
8 flour tortillas (8-inch)
2 cups shredded lettuce (about ½ small
    head)

1. In medium skillet over medium-high heat, cook beef until browned, stirring to separate meat. Pour off fat.

2. Add soup and salsa. Reduce heat to low and heat through.

3. Spoon *about ⅓ cup* meat mixture down center of each tortilla. Top with lettuce. Fold tortilla around filling. Serve with additional salsa. *Makes 4 servings*

Prep/Cook Time: 15 minutes

TERIYAKI BURGERS

1 pound ground beef
3 tablespoons *French's*® Teriyaki Grill &
    Glaze Sauce

1. Combine beef with **Grill & Glaze** Sauce. Shape into 4 burgers.

2. Broil or grill burgers 10 minutes or until no longer pink in center, basting with additional **Grill & Glaze** Sauce. *Makes 4 servings*

Prep Time: 5 minutes
Cook Time: 15 minutes

Beefy Bean & Walnut Stir-Fry

RICE-STUFFED PEPPERS

1 package LIPTON® Rice & Sauce—
    Cheddar Broccoli
2 cups water
1 tablespoon margarine or butter
1 pound ground beef
4 large red or green bell peppers, halved
    lengthwise and seeded

Preheat oven to 350°F.

Prepare rice & sauce—cheddar broccoli with water and margarine according to package directions.

Meanwhile, in 10-inch skillet, brown ground beef over medium-high heat; drain. Stir into rice & sauce. Fill each pepper half with rice mixture. In 13×9-inch baking dish, arrange stuffed peppers. Bake covered 20 minutes. Remove cover and continue baking 10 minutes or until peppers are tender. Sprinkle, if desired, with shredded cheddar cheese.

Makes about 4 main-dish servings

MAGIC TIP

Select bell peppers that are firm and heavy in proportion to their size, with shiny skin and a robust color. Avoid peppers with wrinkled or limp skin, soft spots or bruises.

MAIN-DISH PIE

1 package (8 rolls) refrigerated crescent
    rolls
1 pound lean ground beef
1 medium onion, chopped
1 can (12 ounces) beef or mushroom gravy
1 box (10 ounces) BIRDS EYE® frozen
    Green Peas, thawed
½ cup shredded Swiss cheese
6 slices tomato

• Preheat oven to 350°F.

• Unroll dough and separate rolls. Spread to cover bottom of ungreased 9-inch pie pan. Press together to form lower crust. Bake 10 minutes.

• Meanwhile, in large skillet, brown beef and onion; drain excess fat.

• Stir in gravy and peas; cook until heated through.

• Pour mixture into partially baked crust. Sprinkle with cheese.

• Bake 10 to 15 minutes or until crust is brown and cheese is melted.

• Arrange tomato slices over pie; bake 2 minutes more.   *Makes 6 servings*

Prep Time: 10 minutes
Cook Time: 20 to 25 minutes

SPEEDY BEEF & BEAN BURRITOS

8 (7-inch) flour tortillas
1 pound ground beef
1 cup chopped onion
1 teaspoon bottled minced garlic
1 can (15 ounces) black beans, drained
    and rinsed
1 cup spicy thick and chunky salsa
2 teaspoons ground cumin
1 bunch cilantro
2 cups (8 ounces) shredded cojack or
    Monterey Jack cheese

1. Wrap tortillas in foil; place on center rack in oven. Heat oven to 350°F; heat tortillas 15 minutes.

2. While tortillas are warming, prepare burrito filling. Combine beef, onion and garlic in large skillet; cook over medium-high heat until beef is no longer pink, breaking beef apart with wooden spoon. Pour off drippings.

3. Stir beans, salsa and cumin into beef mixture; reduce heat to medium. Cover and simmer 10 minutes, stirring once.

4. While filling is simmering, chop enough cilantro to measure ¼ cup. Stir into filling. Spoon filling down centers of warm tortillas; top with cheese. Roll up and serve immediately.

Makes 4 servings

Prep and Cook Time: 20 minutes

BISTRO BURGERS WITH BLUE CHEESE

1 pound ground beef or turkey
¼ cup chopped fresh parsley
2 tablespoons minced chives
¼ teaspoon dried thyme leaves
2 tablespoons *French's®* Dijon Mustard
    Lettuce and tomato slices
4 crusty rolls, split in half
2 ounces blue cheese, crumbled
1⅓ cups *French's® Taste Toppers*™ French
    Fried Onions

1. In large bowl, gently mix meat, herbs and mustard. Shape into 4 patties.

2. Grill or broil patties 10 minutes or until no longer pink in center. Arrange lettuce and tomatoes on bottom halves of rolls. Place burgers on top. Sprinkle with blue cheese and *Taste Toppers*. Cover with top halves of rolls. Serve with additional mustard.

Toast *Taste Toppers* in microwave 1 minute for extra crispness.

Makes 4 servings

Prep Time: 10 minutes
Cook Time: 10 minutes

Speedy Beef & Bean Burritos

The publisher would like to thank the companies and organizations listed below for the use of their recipes and photographs in this publication.

A.1.® Steak Sauce

Birds Eye®

Campbell Soup Company

Del Monte Corporation

The Golden Grain Company®

The HV Company

Kraft Foods Holdings

Lawry's® Foods, Inc.

Lipton®

McIlhenny Company (TABASCO® brand Pepper Sauce)

Nestlé USA, Inc.

North Dakota Beef Commission

North Dakota Wheat Commission

The Quaker® Oatmeal Kitchens

Reckitt Benckiser

RED STAR® Yeast & Products, A Division of SENSIENT TECHNOLOGIES CORPORATION

Riviana Foods Inc.

Sonoma® Dried Tomatoes

The Fremont Company, Makers of Frank's & SnowFloss Kraut and Tomato Products

Uncle Ben's Inc.

USA Dry Pea & Lentil Council

Wisconsin Milk Marketing Board

Albóndigas Soup, 58
All-in-One Burger Stew, 72
Artichoke Casserole, 30

Beans
  Beefy Bean & Walnut Stir-Fry, 88
  Campbell's® Quick Beef 'n' Beans Tacos, 10
  Campbell's® Southwest Skillet, 55
  Crunchy Layered Beef & Bean Salad, 76
  Durango Chili, 64
  Fast 'n' Easy Chili, 78
  First Alarm Chili, 78
  Meaty Chili, 71
  Mexican Vegetable Beef Soup, 60
  Monterey Black Bean Tortilla Supper, 36
  Quick & Easy Chili, 62
  Rapid Ragú® Chili, 68
  Riverboat Chili, 72
  Second Alarm Chili, 78
  Speedy Beef & Bean Burritos, 84
  Spicy Quick and Easy Chili, 65
  Taco Pot Pie, 52
  Tamale Pie, 38
  Tex-Mex Beef & Black Bean Skillet, 50
  Third Alarm Chili, 78
Beef & Zucchini Quiche, 37
Beef Stroganoff Casserole, 26
Beefy Bean & Walnut Stir-Fry, 88
Beefy Nacho Crescent Bake, 24
Bistro Burgers with Blue Cheese, 84
Bite Size Tacos, 86
Broccoli and Beef Pasta, 56

California Tamale Pie, 26
Campbell's® Beef & Cheddar Soft Tacos, 88
Campbell's® Beef & Mozzarella Bake, 32
Campbell's® Beefy Macaroni Skillet, 52
Campbell's® Country Skillet Supper, 48
Campbell's® Country Skillet Supper Provençal, 48
Campbell's® Easy Skillet Beef & Hash Browns, 80
Campbell's® Fiesta Taco Salad, 8
Campbell's® Quick Beef 'n' Beans Tacos, 10

Campbell's® Quick Beef Skillet, 87
Campbell's® Southwest Skillet, 55
Campbell's® Spicy Salsa Mac & Beef, 49
Carrots
  Albóndigas Soup, 58
  Campbell's® Quick Beef Skillet, 87
  Classic Meatball Soup, 66
  Szechwan Beef, 54
Cheeseburger Macaroni, 48
Chili Beef Mac, 66
Chilies
  Durango Chili, 64
  Meaty Chili, 71
  Mexican Stuffed Shells, 34
  Quick & Easy Chili, 62
  Spicy Quick and Easy Chili, 65
  Texas Beef Stew, 62
  Texas-Style Chili, 70
Chuckwagon BBQ Rice Round-Up, 42
Classic Meatball Soup, 66
Contadina® Classic Lasagne, 18
Corn
  California Tamale Pie, 26
  Chuckwagon BBQ Rice Round-Up, 42
  Corny Sloppy Joes, 86
  Farmer's Stew Argentina, 70
  Groovy Angel Hair Goulash, 82
  Southwestern Meat Loaf, 16
  Spicy Quick and Easy Chili, 65
  Szechwan Beef, 54
  Taco Pot Pie, 52
  Texas Beef Stew, 62
  Western Wagon Wheels, 55
Corny Sloppy Joes, 86
Creamy Beef and Vegetable Casserole, 78
Crunchy Layered Beef & Bean Salad, 76
Curry Beef, 50

Deep Dish All-American Pizza, 10
Durango Chili, 64

Easy Mostaccioli Casserole, 8

Farmer's Stew Argentina, 70
Fast 'n' Easy Chili, 78
First Alarm Chili, 78
Four-Cheese Lasagna, 12

Greek Beef & Rice, 46
Greek-Style Lasagna, 38
Grilled Meat Loaves and Potatoes, 22
Groovy Angel Hair Goulash, 82

Hanoi Beef and Rice Soup, 65
Heartland Shepherd's Pie, 40
Hearty Beef Stew, 64
Hearty Chili Mac, 60

Italian Beef Burrito, 46

Joe's Special, 44

Lasagna Beef 'n' Spinach Roll-Ups, 40
Lasagna Roll-Ups, 22
Lasagna Supreme, 20
Lipton® Onion Burgers, 20

Main-Dish Pie, 90
Malaysian Curried Beef, 28
Manicotti Parmigiana, 11
Meaty Chili, 71
Mediterranean Burgers, 14
Mexican Stuffed Shells, 34
Mexican Vegetable Beef Soup, 60
Minestrone Soup with Mini Meatballs, 68
Mini Meat Loaves & Vegetables, 19
Mini Mexican Burger Bites, 80
Monterey Black Bean Tortilla Supper, 36
Moussaka, 36
Mushrooms
  Artichoke Casserole, 30
  Beef Stroganoff Casserole, 26
  Deep Dish All-American Pizza, 10
  Joe's Special, 44
  Lasagna Supreme, 20
  Quick Beef Stroganoff, 56
  Salsbury Steaks with Mushroom-Wine Sauce, 74
  Spinach-Potato Bake, 28

Nacho Bacho, 87

Olives
  California Tamale Pie, 26
  Easy Mostaccioli Casserole, 8
  Mediterranean Burgers, 14
  Nacho Bacho, 87
  Quick Greek Pitas, 54

Pasta
All-in-One Burger Stew, 72
Beef Stroganoff Casserole, 26
Broccoli and Beef Pasta, 56
Campbell's® Beefy Macaroni
Skillet, 52
Campbell's® Beef & Mozzarella
Bake, 32
Campbell's® Country Skillet
Supper, 48
Campbell's® Country Skillet
Supper Provençal, 48
Campbell's® Spicy Salsa Mac &
Beef, 49
Cheeseburger Macaroni, 48
Chili Beef Mac, 66
Classic Meatball Soup, 66
Contadina® Classic Lasagne,
18
Curry Beef, 50
Easy Mostaccioli Casserole, 8
Four-Cheese Lasagna, 12
Groovy Angel Hair Goulash, 82
Hearty Chili Mac, 60
Lasagna Beef 'n' Spinach Roll-
Ups, 40
Lasagna Roll-Ups, 22
Lasagna Supreme, 20
Manicotti Parmigiana, 11
Mexican Stuffed Shells, 34
Pasta "Pizza," 29
Pasta Beef & Zucchini Dinner,
49
Prego® Baked Ziti Supreme, 14
Prego® Easy Spaghetti &
Meatballs, 16
Quick Beef Stroganoff, 56
Ragú® Chili Mac, 44
String Pie, 34
Tacos in Pasta Shells, 30
Western Wagon Wheels, 55
Peppers, Bell (*see also* **Chilies**)
Chili Beef Mac, 66
Contadina® Classic Lasagne,
18
Deep Dish All-American Pizza,
10
Durango Chili, 64
Farmer's Stew Argentina, 70
Italian Beef Burrito, 46
Mini Mexican Burger Bites, 80
Pasta "Pizza," 29
Pizza Meat Loaf, 6
Polynesian Burgers, 12
Quick 'n' Easy Tacos, 79
Ragú® Chili Mac, 44
Rice-Stuffed Peppers, 90

Riverboat Chili, 72
Saucy Stuffed Peppers, 19
Southwestern Meat Loaf, 16
Stuffed Mexican Pizza Pie, 37
Texas-Style Chili, 70
Western Hash, 87
Pizza Meat Loaf, 6
Polynesian Burgers, 12
Potatoes
Albóndigas Soup, 58
Campbell's® Easy Skillet Beef
& Hash Browns, 80
Campbell's® Quick Beef Skillet,
87
Farmer's Stew Argentina, 70
Grilled Meat Loaves and
Potatoes, 22
Hearty Beef Stew, 64
Malaysian Curried Beef, 28
Mini Meat Loaves &
Vegetables, 19
Moussaka, 36
Spinach-Potato Bake, 28
Taco Taters, 80
Texas Beef Stew, 62
Prego® Baked Ziti Supreme, 14
Prego® Easy Spaghetti &
Meatballs, 16

Quick & Easy Chili, 62
Quick 'n' Easy Tacos, 79
Quick Beef Stroganoff, 56
Quick Greek Pitas, 54

Ragú® Chili Mac, 44
Ranch Lentil Casserole, 34
Rapid Ragú® Chili, 68
Rice
Albóndigas Soup, 58
Campbell's® Southwest Skillet,
55
Chuckwagon BBQ Rice Round-
Up, 42
Farmer's Stew Argentina, 70
Greek Beef & Rice, 46
Hanoi Beef and Rice Soup, 65
Malaysian Curried Beef, 28
Rice-Stuffed Peppers, 90
Special Occasion Meat Loaf, 11
Stuffed Mexican Pizza Pie, 37
Sweet and Sour Beef, 82
Szechwan Beef, 54
Tex-Mex Beef & Black Bean
Skillet, 50
Western Hash, 87
Wild Rice Soup, 71
Riverboat Chili, 72

Salsbury Steaks with Mushroom-
Wine Sauce, 74
Saucy Stuffed Peppers, 19
Sausage
Lasagna Supreme, 20
Meaty Chili, 71
Special Occasion Meat Loaf, 11
Second Alarm Chili, 78
Shepherd's Pie, 32
Sloppy Joe Rollers, 79
Sloppy Onion Joes, 12
Sonoma Burgers Stuffed with
Blue Cheese, 76
Southwestern Meat Loaf, 16
Special Occasion Meat Loaf, 11
Speedy Beef & Bean Burritos, 84
Spicy Quick and Easy Chili, 65
Spinach
Joe's Special, 44
Lasagna Beef 'n' Spinach Roll-
Ups, 40
Quick Greek Pitas, 54
Special Occasion Meat Loaf, 11
Spinach-Potato Bake, 28
String Pie, 34
Stuffed Mexican Pizza Pie, 37
Sweet and Sour Beef, 82
Szechwan Beef, 54

Taco Pot Pie, 52
Tacos in Pasta Shells, 30
Taco Taters, 80
Tamale Pie, 38
Tempting Taco Burgers, 18
Teriyaki Burgers, 88
Texas Beef Stew, 62
Texas-Style Chili, 70
Tex-Mex Beef & Black Bean
Skillet, 50
Third Alarm Chili, 78

Western Hash, 87
Western Wagon Wheels, 55
Wild Rice Soup, 71

Zucchini
Beef & Zucchini Quiche, 37
Campbell's® Country Skillet
Supper, 48
Campbell's® Country Skillet
Supper Provençal, 48
Farmer's Stew Argentina, 70
Greek Beef & Rice, 46
Moussaka, 36
Pasta Beef & Zucchini Dinner,
49
Zucchini Lasagne, 29

METRIC CONVERSION CHART

VOLUME
MEASUREMENTS (dry)

$1/8$ teaspoon = 0.5 mL
$1/4$ teaspoon = 1 mL
$1/2$ teaspoon = 2 mL
$3/4$ teaspoon = 4 mL
1 teaspoon = 5 mL
1 tablespoon = 15 mL
2 tablespoons = 30 mL
$1/4$ cup = 60 mL
$1/3$ cup = 75 mL
$1/2$ cup = 125 mL
$2/3$ cup = 150 mL
$3/4$ cup = 175 mL
1 cup = 250 mL
2 cups = 1 pint = 500 mL
3 cups = 750 mL
4 cups = 1 quart = 1 L

VOLUME MEASUREMENTS (fluid)

1 fluid ounce (2 tablespoons) = 30 mL
4 fluid ounces ($1/2$ cup) = 125 mL
8 fluid ounces (1 cup) = 250 mL
12 fluid ounces ($1½$ cups) = 375 mL
16 fluid ounces (2 cups) = 500 mL

WEIGHTS (mass)

$1/2$ ounce = 15 g
1 ounce = 30 g
3 ounces = 90 g
4 ounces = 120 g
8 ounces = 225 g
10 ounces = 285 g
12 ounces = 360 g
16 ounces = 1 pound = 450 g

DIMENSIONS

$1/16$ inch = 2 mm
$1/8$ inch = 3 mm
$1/4$ inch = 6 mm
$1/2$ inch = 1.5 cm
$3/4$ inch = 2 cm
1 inch = 2.5 cm

OVEN
TEMPERATURES

250°F = 120°C
275°F = 140°C
300°F = 150°C
325°F = 160°C
350°F = 180°C
375°F = 190°C
400°F = 200°C
425°F = 220°C
450°F = 230°C

BAKING PAN SIZES

Utensil	Size in Inches/Quarts	Metric Volume	Size in Centimeters
Baking or Cake Pan (square or rectangular)	8×8×2	2 L	20×20×5
	9×9×2	2.5 L	23×23×5
	12×8×2	3 L	30×20×5
	13×9×2	3.5 L	33×23×5
Loaf Pan	8×4×3	1.5 L	20×10×7
	9×5×3	2 L	23×13×7
Round Layer Cake Pan	8×1½	1.2 L	20×4
	9×1½	1.5 L	23×4
Pie Plate	8×1¼	750 mL	20×3
	9×1¼	1 L	23×3
Baking Dish or Casserole	1 quart	1 L	—
	1½ quart	1.5 L	—
	2 quart	2 L	—